motherhood is Easy....

..as long as you have nothing else to do for the next 50 years.

REBEKAH HUNTER SCOTT
ILLUSTRATIONS BY CARRIE HUNTER

© 2010 ClearView Press

Motherhood is Easy: As Long You Have Nothing Else To Do For The Next 50 Years
Copyright © 2010 by Rebekah Hunter Scott
Cover Design & Illustrations by Carrie Hunter. All rights reserved.
Copy Editor Amy H. Dutta

Scott, Rebekah Hunter
      Motherhood is Easy: As Long You Have Nothing Else To Do For The Next 50 Years
      192 p. ill. cm.
      ISBN 978-0-9799623-3-2 (sc)   978-0-9799623-4-9 (ebook)
      1. Parenting—Motherhood—Relationships.   I. Title.
HQ756
649.1
Library of Congress Control Number: 2010922623

All Rights Reserved. No part of this book may be reproduced, stored in a retrieval system, or transmitted in any form or by any means, electronic, mechanical, photocopying, recording, or otherwise, without permission in writing from ClearView Press, Inc.

ClearView Press, Inc.
PO Box 353431
Palm Coast, FL 32135-3431
www.clearviewpressinc.com

Printed in the United States of America

The Experts on *Motherhood Is Easy*....

"Typically, a book about mommyhood is not a page turner, but *Motherhood is Easy* is. Rebekah Hunter Scott elevates white trash baby-raising to a soulful level. What can I say? Laughing out loud, chapter for chapter, covers a lot of sins."
  -Suzette Martinez Standring, Columnist, GateHouse News Service, Milton, MA

"You will laugh as you remember similar happenings along your child-rearing path. If you want to smile and feel a kinship to females everywhere, read this book in its entirety! You will be glad you did!"
  - Patricia Palmer Johnson, retired mother of two, Gardenerville, NV

"This book is a comforting, brilliantly funny reminder that all moms experience the same trials and tribulations of motherhood, and that a considerable dose of humor helps you survive it! Whether you're a brand-new parent or already up to your armpits in dirty diapers, spilled juice and runny noses, you'll be able to laugh and commiserate along with these wonderfully honest and hilarious anecdotes."
  -Gina Rundle, graphic designer and mother of three, Sycamore, IL

"This book reads like a conversation with your best friend! The tales provide comic relief to a mom's daily life."
  -Erin Lind, instructor and mother of two, Jacksonville, FL

"Rebekah Hunter Scott nails it with this book! Who can't identify with motherhood mishaps? I laughed out loud as I was reading it and I laugh out loud just thinking about it. It's a must-read for any mother."
  -Laila Murphy, musician and mother of two, Lake Oswego, OR

"Rebekah Hunter Scott's hugely funny and relevant book about motherhood will have you turning page after page. Reading this book, we want to know what happens next while realizing these are not mere characters from a novel. This is real life! If you have children or have ever thought of having children, this book is a must-read!"
  -Guinevere Edern, author of *Among Other Edens*, Altamonte Springs, FL

The Experts on *Motherhood Is Easy*....

"What a delightful read! Curling up with Motherhood is Easy and a cup of tea while the little one is napping is the perfect prescription for momma's composure!"
-Helen Drake King, mother of four, Dunbar, WV

"With a voice as refreshing and delightful as Sex on the Beach (the real thing, not the cocktail) Rebekah Hunter Scott nails what it feels like to have that special love-hate relationship with your kids and husband that only a mommy can have...When Rebekah writes about embracing your "Inner White Trash" while at Wal-Mart with a kid wearing only a diaper and trying to buy a pair of shorts because you had forgotten to pack them in your diaper bag… I can relate.

"While I have never been able to relate to the moms out there who have matching baby accessories, video cameras focused on their sleeping cherubs, and who know how to effectively remove every stain known to mankind from their children's clothing, I am able to relate to a funny, sharp witted, intelligent, and honest mom who realizes that while she loves her children, being a mom is a tough, tough job that —without humor—can crush even the strongest woman.

"With great insight, Rebekah Hunter Scott shares with us her battle stories of mommy-hood from deep in the trenches – poopy diapers, dried lady bug carcasses and all. She will make you laugh, she'll make you cry, she'll make you realize that you're not alone when, at the end of the day, you decide that alcohol is enough of a food pyramid for you."
-Wendy Thomas, BookPleasures.com

Acknowledgements

Thank you, Mike, for planting this crazy seed in my brain in the first place. You took a chance on me before you even knew if I could write my way out of a wet paper bag. A million times, thank you.

Thank you, Jeff Swesky and Tracy McDurmon, the remaining Rogues Gallery Writers, for all the laughter, encouragement, and beers. You guys are truly gifted, patient, and freaking hilarious. And thank you, Bobbie, for your hard work and guidance through this project—you truly are a Super Woman.

Thank you, my wonderful, wonderful Saint Augustine Moms, for keeping my sanity relatively in-check. A special thanks to Lindy, Sarah B., Jen R. and Emily for being my reading Guinea Pigs (and for still talking to me after reading it).

Thank you, Suzette, Laila, Aunt Patti, Gina, Erin, Helen, and Jenny, for giving me a few hours of your life. Your kind words are invaluable.

Thank you to my family, for helping shape my twisted sense of humor through years of dysfunctional hilarity. I shudder to think what I would be like without car trouble on road trips, Hunt The Wumpus, stale popcorn, the hose caddy, eight people in a VW Bug, The Mustache Man, or Reaux-Sham-Beaux. I love you all. If we were all stranded on a desert island, however, I'd probably vote to eat Evan first…he would be the most nutritious.

Thank you, Lish, for being eternally supportive and effusively optimistic. I'm your Number One Fan, and likewise, I'm sure.

Thank you, Amy, for just being Amy. Kidding! I would trust you with my grammatical life. And thank yo=u for being The Octopus, if only for a few years.

Thank you, Carrie. I'm pretty sure you know why, but I'll tell you anyway…your artistic brilliance is overwhelming. Thank you for keeping me as un-cheesy and wise-looking as possible. You rule, and I am just a Mr. Cornflake.

Thank you, Jeff, for always, always believing in me. I love you.

For Jeff…for getting his chocolate in my peanut butter.

And for Rollie and Elsa…our peanut butter cups.

"Making the decision to have a child is momentous. It is to decide forever to have your heart go walking around outside your body." ~Elizabeth Stone

"Mothers are all slightly insane." ~ J.D. Salinger

Table of Contents

Introduction

Chapter 1: He Got His Chocolate In My Peanut Butter 17

Chapter 2: First Children Are Destined For Greatness And All Subsequent Children Can Suck It 23

Chapter 3: Tell Us How You Really Feel 33

Chapter 4: Thirty-Pound Birth Control 39

Chapter 5: No Shirt, No Shoes, No Shame 43

Chapter 6: Why 'Because I Said So' Is A Perfectly Acceptable Reason 49

Chapter 7: I Do Anal 55

Chapter 8: Naptime (aka: Let's See How Many Facebook Walls I Can Write On Before They Wake Up) 61

Chapter 9: Step Away From The Scissors 67

Chapter 10: Are Children No Longer Starving In China? 71

Chapter 11: Playdate Etiquette (aka: Let's Vacuum The House In A Full-On Sprint Ten Minutes Before The Doorbell Rings—It's Great Cardio) 77

Chapter 12: Excuse Me, But Your Nipple Is Showing 81

Chapter 13: The Octopus And The Butterfly 87

Chapter 14: The Switch 93

Chapter 15: The Incredible Journey—To The Grocery Store 99

Chapter 16: I Spy A Bar—Be Right Back, Kids 107

Chapter 17: Liar Liar, Diaper On Fire 115

Chapter 18: Levels Of Consciousness Not Achieved With Chemical Substances 123

Chapter 19: Guide To Half-Assed Cleaning 131

Chapter 20: Apple Dapple Purse 137

Chapter 21: The Quick And...The Not-So-Quick 143

Chapter 22: In Summary 149

Extra Laughs From Online 151

Introduction

In the beginning, there was Man and Woman.

Then there was Alcohol and Lapses in Judgment.

Then there were Children.

This book is for those of you who have removed Play-doh from a human orifice, who have enough batteries in your house to power a small country for several weeks, or who have had someone under three feet tall announce in a public restroom that he sees your poopy in the toilet.

Kids do some funny stuff. I'll give them that. They're like prop comics. The other day I watched my son brush his hair with a lollipop. I've seen him use the TV remote as a baseball bat. I've seen him try to stick a bobby pin in his ear (and I leapt across the room like Baryshnikov to prevent a trip to the emergency room). Their creative well never runs dry.

I realize that being a mom is a sacred thing. I realize how lucky I am to be one. Just keep that in mind, because for the next one hundred-odd pages, it may seem like I loathe my children, and would rather be a professional earthworm wrangler than a stay-at-home mother of a son with contact dermatitis and a daughter who thinks the bathtub is a toilet. But I wouldn't trade them for anything in world. Except maybe a granite countertop.

My sister Amy who once told me "Motherhood is Easy…as long as you have absolutely nothing else to do for the next 50 years. Like, you know… breathe, sleep, eat, have sex. If you don't mind going without those things for a while, motherhood is a cakewalk."

Otherwise it's…well…interesting. Sometimes it sucks. Sometimes it's messy, smelly, irritating, tedious, draining, and mind-blowingly challenging. It can drive you to scream, cry, drink, and convince you that you're losing your mind. And just when you think you've got it figured out, it throws you a big, fat curve ball.

And it's worth it. No, really. It's worth it. But we're going to need to find strength somewhere if we're going to survive this. My solution is to laugh.

Long, hard, and often.

Chapter 1
He Got His Chocolate In My Peanut Butter

Pregnancy.

The very word used to make my ovaries quake in fear and dread. In my early days of sexual activity, I peed on my fair share of plastic sticks, hoping and praying and bargaining with God to please please *please* let me see a little negative sign in the window, a tinge of pink on the TP. Please let me be bitchy because of PMS and not because I have a surge of hCG in my veins.

And what a relief it was to discover I'd dodged another bullet, skated through one more month. I laughed out loud as I sat in the bathroom, and vowed to be a little more responsible next time. I kept chugging along to my childless soundtrack, dancing through life carefree and unfettered.

Then the soundtrack changed from house music to something that sounded oddly like *Twinkle, Twinkle Little Star*. Inevitably, the very thing I'd been threatened with and warned about for years and years was finally something I suddenly wanted and deserved to have. Pregnancy was a promise instead of a

Week 27

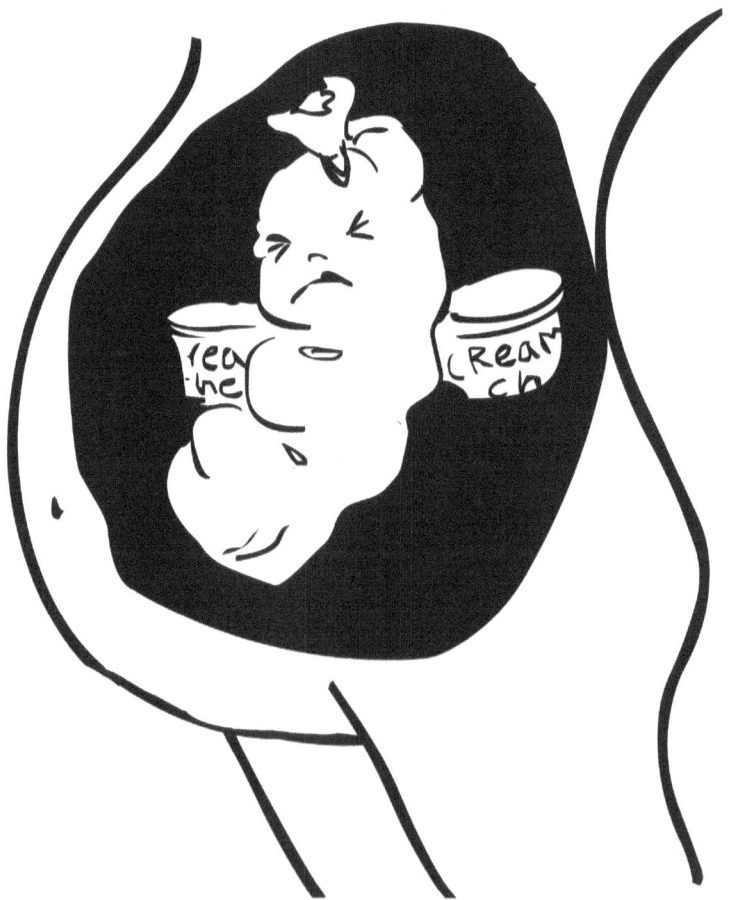

portent, a blessing instead of a plague. Now I slowed down a little as I walked past Baby Gap, I peeked inside of strollers and cooed at the gummy smiles of strangers' babies. Instead of internally groaning at the sight of a mother holding an infant as we boarded the same airplane, I felt my own arms ache to be the one holding a chubby, squirming, babbling bundle of baby. Tick tock, tick tock, tick tock….

    I sure didn't expect getting knocked up to take so freaking long. The way my high school made it seem, if a guy so much as shared his can of soda with you, you were pretty much guaranteed a teenage pregnancy (see Chapter 4, Thirty-Pound Birth Control). But after a few unsuccessful years of working in the kitchen and still not getting a bun in the oven, my husband Jeff and I had some tests run. I bought one of those ovulation predictor kits. Jeff spent one particularly frantic and embarrassing fifteen minutes in the backseat of our car as I sped to the, um…the lab (I guess doing it in the car is better than sitting in a private room with a bunch of backdated *Playboys*). We went through the gamut of emotions typical of most couples who are bumping uglies for anything other than recreational purposes. Anger. Confusion. Frustration. And a little rueful that we didn't, you know, have a lot more sex, since getting pregnant isn't quite as easy as someone getting his chocolate in your peanut butter.

    After the tests claimed that we had nothing wrong with our baby-making equipment, we went through this phase where we tried to better ourselves as human beings—I started piano, he started learning German, and we could both run a six-minute mile (why that made us better human beings I'm not sure, but I could play *Claire De Lune*, he could understand *Das Boot* without subtitles and we had us a pair of very firm, taut little asses). We traveled, watched movies, hung out and sort of mentally drummed our fingers as we waited for something to happen.

    And then…Holy Crap, we're gonna have a baby.

It took a while to sink in. In that while, I realized that I wouldn't be able to drink for nine whole months. And I was gonna get fat. And I was gonna get *boobs* (hey, now that didn't sound so bad). I'm glad I was so self-indulgent while I had the chance—that was the last time it was all about me.

I spent the first few months of pregnancy on the couch with the shades drawn, watching Seinfeld reruns and trying not to vomit. I slept a lot, ate cannolis and cereal when I felt like eating, and read a few of those books like, *Your Pregnancy Week by Week*. Let me tell you that those weeks really crawled by. I think I read *What To Expect When You're Expecting* in its entirety before my baby's eyes had moved to the front of his head. I had a tadpole and I was ready for a little person.

(Side note: For some reason, books and websites about pregnancy always compare your baby to a random fruit or vegetable. *Week Fourteen – your baby now resembles a large lemon. Week Twenty-One – your baby is about the size and shape of a spaghetti squash.* Or my favorite, *Week Thirty-Nine – your baby is as large as a medium-sized pumpkin.* At that point, can't they just say, your baby is the size and shape of a seven-pound baby? What would have been helpful was if the writers had compared a growing baby to starches, my preferred food group. *Week Twenty-Seven – your baby is as big as a package of bagels and a few tubs of cream cheese. Week Thirty-Two – your baby is a box of Lucky Charms and several sleeves of Ritz Crackers.* Now *that* would give me a better idea of size. I can't think of the last time I even *looked* at a spaghetti squash.)

So I was trucking along, hitting my pregnancy stride, incubating a baby that was swiftly moving up the ranks of the food pyramid. He kicked, he squirmed, my belly wobbled like Jell-o when he was awake and pushing around in there. I approached the due date feeling relatively educated and somewhat ready to shove him out into the world. How bad could it be, really? We went to a birthing class, saw the videos, looked at the diagrams, and practiced breathing. None of it was too daunting. I had a fairly high threshold of pain and a low set of expectations for the Big Day. As long as I went into the hospital pregnant and left with a baby, I figured I'd be fine.

Cue lightning crash and maniacal, Vincent-Price-esque laughter.

I won't go into the whole birthing experience, because doing it justice would require more pages than I care to designate here. I will say two things, though—giving birth is nuts, and drugs are good. I highly recommend taking drugs.

Especially once your child turns two.

Chapter 2
First Children Are Destined For Greatness and All Subsequent Children Can Suck It

And so, with our bun finally baking away in the oven, Jeff and I crossed over into the Land Of First-Time Parents.

You can spot First-Time Parents a mile away. They wander around Babies-R-Us armed with those scan-guns, tentatively aiming it at every piece of baby gear within a five-foot radius like they're at a shooting gallery. Wipe warmers, pacifier cases, his and hers diaper bags, little tiny pairs of Nikes—they load up on everything they think they could possibly need, everything they didn't even *know* they needed, and everything they didn't even know *existed*.

When we registered for the first time at Babies-R-Us, my older sister Amy came with us. We needed her as a consultant to help us navigate the fifty different kinds of bottles, bibs, strollers and play pens (or, excuse me, pack-and-plays, since the name 'play pen' is apparently politically incorrect—a child who sleeps in a 'play pen' is likely to commit his first felony by the age of ten).

First Time Parents

Who knew something as simple as a pacifier could come in so many different varieties? Rubber nipples, silicone nipples, orthodontist-approved nipples, extra-durable nipples, straight nipples, bi-curious nipples, the list goes on.

At one point during our registration adventure, my husband and I weren't sure what sort of sheet we needed for the pack-and-play-pen. We discussed our options, finally going with one that matched the design on the crib itself.

I turned to Amy for her blessing, and she was just shaking her head.

"What?" I asked.

"You guys are such first parents," she said.

"What's that supposed to mean?" I asked. I was eight months pregnant and at the point where I took everything the wrong way. Seriously. Tell me it's a nice day and I automatically take that to mean I look fat.

"Nothing," she said. "It's not in a bad way. It's just…funny."

"Funny how?"

All she could do was shrug. "You'll see."

She was right, of course. You do a lot of hand-wringing, fretting, vacillating, pondering, and that's before the baby even *arrives*. Even the most laid-back, easy-going of us spends entirely too much time agonizing over nursery themes and bottle types, wondering if the wrong decision will turn what would have been the next Bill Gates or Michael Jordon into a whiny little dumb-ass.

But on the upside, you also marvel at that first one. A lot. Marvel at little hands and feet, little mouths, little noses, little eyebrows…. Even at your most sleep-deprived, you still appreciate that you are now a parent. There's a reason you only get four hours of crappy, sporadic sleep at night. There's a reason you have to sit on a pillow shaped like a donut, that your boobs are bigger than your head and twice as hard, that you smuggled several of those giant pairs of granny panties from the hospital (not only are they the *sexiest* pair of underwear you'll ever own, but they're also the most comfortable). You have a little person completely at your mercy.

You spend hours assembling birth announcements to trumpet to the world about your first-born child. You lie on the couch with him curled up on your chest (isn't that the best?). You strain your ears to hear the tiniest little squeaks and grunts. Even his raspy cries of hunger or discomfort are sweeter than any song.

You *also* change a crapload of diapers.

So was anyone else surprised to learn that babies can poop clear across a room? Looking at a tiny, newborn baby, you wouldn't think they were capable of such deadly force. They especially like doing this at two in the morning, when you're even more bleary-eyed, fuzzy-headed and vulnerable than usual. One minute you're changing an innocuous, wet diaper, so looking forward to lying back down in your bed and feeling the bone-tired agony drain away like you're sweating it out into your mattress. The next minute, with perhaps only a second or two of rumbling in your baby's tummy as a warning, you hear an awful sound, like someone violently squirting ketchup onto a hotdog. Only you know it's not ketchup, and it doesn't land on a hotdog. It lands everywhere but on a hotdog. The changing table, the wall, the floor, you can feel some on your leg. It's everywhere. Just when you think you got it all, you find more. And you start to wonder if you are somehow blessed with a baby whose lower intestines are bionic.

This happened to me almost nightly. I thought I had the timing down. I thought I'd given him the appropriate amount of time to fill his diaper before I dared open it up and put on a new one. But somehow he knew it. As soon as I had him all cleaned up and ready for the fresh diaper, I would hear the telltale rumbling. And then…Dah dah DAH. The Fountain Of Poop. (And P.S.—I don't care who you are. I don't care if you are seven stories above every kind of low-brow potty humor, or if you grew up amidst royalty and have never so much as smirked at a joke involving bodily functions in your entire life…once you have kids, poop is sort of funny.)

As the months wore on, his digestive tract became a little less ominous, and Rollie turned into a full-fledged, sweet-pea, cutie-pie baby. And I fell in love. I lay on the floor with him, reading books, building towers with blocks that had pictures and letters and numbers on every side, bombarding him with as much educational stimuli as possible—he was learning tactile building skills and his ABC's at once, plus getting in some valuable mom-bonding time, while Beethoven played in the background. All his toys were clean, brand-spanking-new, and age-appropriate (and sometimes I felt like hot shit and bought him a toy for 6 months and up when he was only 4 months old…and when he actually played with it properly, I would rejoice in the fact that I had a prodigy on my hands). I was hyper-aware of every milestone, major (crawling) and minor (the first time he simultaneously peed, sneezed and spit up), and praised him for each as if he'd just discovered a gaping hole in the theory of relativity.

And I took an ungodly number of pictures. Every time he looked cute, smiled wide, or wore a ridiculously adorable outfit, I broke out the camera and snapped away. I probably have one from every day of his first year. At least. Someday I'd like to put together a flipbook and watch him age like a time-lapsed photography clip.

Elsa is a different story. Like most mothers about to have Child Numero Dos, I didn't have a lot of time to dwell on my second pregnancy. Even going into labor had kind of a Been There, Done That feel to it. At the time of this chapter, she's seven months old, and I think she can crawl, but I'm not positive. I mean, I'm pretty sure. I put her down in one place, walk away for a minute and when I come back she's somewhere else. So she's at least somewhat mobile. Either that or she's learned how to teleport. She also

Infant Teleportation

babbles a lot, but that's probably because she thinks she better speak up or I'm liable to toss her in the toy box like a doll whose batteries have died.

I know what she's going through. I myself am the fifth of six children. My oldest sibling Alicia was born in 1967, practically before cameras, and yet tucked away inside my mother's photo albums are pages and pages of Alicia at various stages of babyhood—sitting, eating, crawling, walking, always smiling, always basking in the undivided attention of two doting parents. My mom still likes to brag that Alicia could walk at eight months, recited lines and lines of catechism from memory, knew the words to a hundred songs, tied her own shoes, and translated ancient Greek into modern day English. When I ask my mother when *I* learned to walk, she says something like, "Oh, you were pretty average…definitely by a year," like she's making it up, can't remember, like I just sort of blend in with the rest of my siblings. I *eventually* learned to walk, of that much she's certain.

So when she was growing up, Alicia was dubbed 'precocious.' And not to sound bitter, but if my mom had nothing to do but finger-walk *my* ass around the house all day long when I was eight months old, I'd probably have been translating Greek in my toddler years, too. Just as Rollie can currently kick a soccer ball like a ten-year-old and has a more extensive vocabulary than some adults I know, Elsa is destined to eke out as best she can. She tags along like a groupie, at the mercy of Rollie's schedule, or mine.

She *is* only a baby. It's not like I can sign her up for ballet or tennis lessons quite yet. But I know that her baby book is collecting dust on her hand-me-down dresser. I'm pretty sure I updated it to reflect, uh, her birth. But that's pretty much it. She was born, she's done some stuff. I've taken a picture here and there, so at least she'll know she existed. But I'm not the parental paparazzi I was with Rollie. I can't create a flipbook of her life. There will be obvious gaps in her development where she'll wonder, *so I went from crawling to prom night?* Talk about precocious.

I was alone with Elsa the other day. It was one of those Blue Moon afternoons when both my kids actually took synchronized naps and Elsa woke up before Rollie did. And so I brought her into our family room, sat down on the floor with her and we just kind of looked at each other. It was the oddest thing. For about five minutes there, I wasn't even sure what to do. I tried desperately to remember what I was doing with Rollie at her age. Building towers out of blocks? Playing Peek-a-boo? Reciting Shakespeare? Phrases like *Object Permanence*, *Tummy Time* and *Independent Play* ran through my head, but I couldn't think of what they meant. I was drawing blanks like a kid on an algebra exam.

I ended up building a tower for her and letting her knock it down, which elicited some great, baby-belly-shaking chuckles. But I still had the nagging sensation that I was doing something wrong, screwing her up somehow, and that this was a feeble attempt to make up for all the time I wasn't spending just with her.

If I ever have any more children (and I used to want five…back when I didn't even have one), I don't know how I'll divide my time. It's bad enough trying to give each kid a fair amount of one-on-one, and that's with only two. I don't know how my parents did it, although I finally understand why I learned about the Birds and the Bees from both whispered giggles on the playground and eavesdropping on my sister and her friend. I mean, my parents sure didn't have time to sit me down and go over anything as involved as s-e-x. As far as they were concerned, the stork brought my siblings and me. And so whatever questions I had regarding technicalities and extenuating details I harvested from wherever I could (which is probably why I've only recently discovered what a *frenulum* is…).

I'm sure plenty of people out there can successfully raise a boatload of children, devote the appropriate amount of time to each one and still maintain their own sanity, but I sure ain't one of them. Maybe I'm too selfish, or paranoid, or just plain old to keep up with a brood of little Jeffs and Rebekahs running around.

And I also got started a little late to have five kids—the generation gap between the last one and me would be a yawning gorge. It would be a shame for my youngest to learn the word *frenulum* from a late-night game of scrabble with his or her spouse.

Chapter 3
Tell Us How You Really Feel

Ever hear someone talking about her children and she says something like, "*Don't get me wrong, I love my son, but I swear to God if he shoves one more raisin into his car seat buckle, I'm going to skin him alive and feed him to his own guinea pig*"?

Why do we feel the need to qualify any derogatory comment about our kids? Are we afraid someone might take our comment the wrong way, call DCF and have our kids whisked away before our disbelieving eyes? Hell, sometimes I *wish* that would happen.

Of *course* we love our children. Sometimes that's the only thing saving them. We love them. We would rather hurl ourselves in front of a large, oncoming truck than see those big, mournful eyes fill with tears, that cherry mouth quiver, that button nose drip even one drop of snot onto our apple juice-stained carpet. If we didn't, they would have been extinguished long ago, on that first, sleep-deprived morning when the coffee-maker decides to malfunction, the cable goes out, the dog barks at the UPS truck and startles awake an infant that had finally, *finally* fallen asleep after being up since three in the morning.

But let's not kid ourselves here. Some days you feel like you no longer know how to speak to your children in anything softer than a 120-decibel screech. Especially if you've spent the majority of the day cleaning bodily fluids off of the floor with a medley of whining, yelling, and British kids singing about Thomas the Train in the background. Factor in that you haven't had a chance to remove your toenail polish—the color that looked so awesome three weeks ago—and now the sight of your chipped Plum Pudding polish is driving you mad and if you have to tell your darling son to get off his baby sister One More Time you swear you're going to scream so loudly you won't be able to speak for a month.

I think you owe it to yourself to vent a little bit.

But I also understand that it's hard not to sound ungrateful when complaining about your kids. I used to be very sensitive to that when I was still trying to get pregnant. I'd hear some mom lamenting about her lack of sleep, her child's tantrums, her propensity to shove her children into the hands of her husband the minute he walked in the door because, dammit, she'd had enough. I used to think how I would never feel that way once I was finally blessed with a kid. I would spend my time relishing in every roll of baby fat, every cry, every smile, every exploded diaper.

Yeah…now that I have kids…not so much.

Don't get me wrong. I love my kids. Really. But after living in that constant, slightly head-throbbing fog in which most mothers operate, I finally get it. I see the other side. The dark side. I understand that one can be grateful and also be exhausted, frustrated, under-sexed, saggy, flabby, hungry and aching for one night of uninterrupted sleep.

For many women I know, one of the best sources of sympathy and understanding comes from the other half of the family equation. The mailman.

Oh, stop, I'm kidding. Of *course* I'm talking about Daddy. No, not *your* daddy.... your *husband*. Remember him? He's the one who got you into this mess, right? The least he could do is hold your hair back while you spew forth complaints about your day.

Sometimes after a particularly trying afternoon, I'll call Jeff around five o'clock, thinking *Please, God, make him be on his way home already* as I speed-dial his cell. I can't tell you what a relief it is to hear the white-noise of traffic in the background when he answers the phone—I can feel the tension leaving my shoulders and suddenly Rollie wiping his nose on the couch and Elsa crawling around with a dirty sock hanging out of her mouth doesn't bother me in the least. I don't even remember the things that drove me completely insane that day. I'm so excited that I'm about to be relieved of my post I chirp that it's been a great day and ask him what he wants for dinner.

If I don't hear that beautiful, beautiful sound of traffic, that's when things get ugly. That's when I start writing more scenes for the running movie script I have in my head. Right now it's sort of like a *Freaky Friday* meets *Mr. Mom* flick. It's loosely autobiographical, of course, but there's also a Sci-Fi element to it—a way for Jeff and I to switch places for one day, or perhaps a week, so we can *really* see whose day is harder.

Unlike most men we know, Jeff truly wishes that he could stay home with the kids while I went out into the world and brought home the bacon. I've asked my friends if their husbands have this same, sick wish, to which most of them shake their heads vigorously, saying something like, "There's no way my husband would last five minutes home with the kids." And while I think Jeff may last a few rounds, I also believe he would wind up face-down on the mat by the end of the day.

Mostly because Jeff hasn't grasped the concept of Marathon Parenting. Like a star going supernova, if Jeff stayed home with the kids, he would burn out and collapse in on himself long before Rollie tried to change his own poopy

The 7-day Switch

diaper, long before Elsa ate a dried ladybug carcass she found in the foyer, long before the dog dug a hole large enough to bury Jimmy Hoffa in the backyard. He can handle the kids in spurts, but I have my doubts that he'd make it from 6 a.m. to 6 p.m. I have the feeling that by 9:50 a.m., right around the time when I try to leave the house to run errands but Elsa decides to take a Monster Truck Dump and Rollie decides it's much more fun to run down lizards on his tricycle than get into the car, Jeff would assume a fetal position and choke to death on his own tears of despair and defeat.

To be fair, I'm sure his day is harder overall. I've no doubt it's heartbreaking to leave every day at the ass-crack of dawn to go make beer. And talk about it. And drink it. And take it home to drink later. What a bitch that must be.

But, until the day comes when he gets home from work with spit-up on his shirt, bite marks on his nipples, the theme song from *Olivia* in his head and utter exhaustion soaking deep in his bones from manhandling fifty pounds of children all day long, the only way we'll know for sure who deserves to sleep in on Saturday is to switch places for a week.

So be on the lookout for *The Seven Day Switch*, coming soon to a theatre near you....

Chapter 4
Thirty-Pound Birth Control

Remember how I was telling you about getting pregnant, and how when I was in high school I was pretty sure anything I did beyond First Base ran me the risk of ending up like one of those girls who wears sweatshirts in summertime to hide her swelling belly? Well, that seed of fear was planted back in high school, when my family moved from New Jersey to the South. I spent my junior and senior years at a small, private, Southern Baptist school.

While my experience in that school is a whoooole other story, during my time there I was required to take a class called Family Development or something like that, which was sort of like a health class in a public school.

Health as in Sex Ed.

As you can imagine, the teacher at my new school did *not* do any demonstrations involving condoms and bananas. I think the actual class on the subject of Sex consisted of the teacher saying something like, *Don't sit on your boyfriend's lap and be a tease, because that will just lead down a path you don't want to*

Teen Contraception

take. That was pretty much it. I guess in a way the intentions were good. Don't do anything that might make your boyfriend even a little bit horny, because we aaaalllll know where that leads. Seems logical. Except that she was giving this speech to a bunch of teenagers, who, like the hypothetical boyfriend in the cautionary tale, were horny. Really, really horny.

Directly following this little lesson in puritanical behavior, we were paired off, boy-girl, and given 5-pound bags of flour with explicit instructions to care for them as if they were babies. I suppose that was another attempt at the school board to squash any desires we may have had to actually engage in any sexual activity. *Have sex, and you, too, will wind up with a sack of flour to lug around for the next nine weeks.*

Needless to say, the lecture on not being a tease, coupled with taking care of an inert bag of flour, did not deter roughly ninety-five percent of the student population from experimenting. (Note to my mom and dad—I was in the five percent who didn't!)

I think where the class went wrong was in the Bag of Flour assignment. A bag of flour in your backpack is not a good form of birth control. If taking care of a bag of flour were ANYTHING like taking care of an actual baby, I can assure you that NO ONE would have had sex at North Florida Christian, or any other school for that matter. I dare you to find one bag of flour, sugar or salt that sucks your nipples raw, cries for absolutely no good reason, goes through fifteen diapers a day, or spits up all over your favorite sweater. Not even the organic, self-rising, all-purpose flour will do that.

Perhaps the school should have rented a bunch of two-year-olds for the class. Because caring for an infant, while demanding in the physical sense, is really just the calm before the storm. The gentle prelude to what will become the most challenging time in a person's life. (I say this having never been a parent of a teenager. I hear I am in for quite an adventure, and I believe every word.) If the class had been required to take care of a toddler, maybe my fellow students wouldn't have ben so quick to sit on each other's laps.

I would have loved to be the teacher in *that* class. Can you imagine assigning a bunch of sixteen-year-olds a day alone with a toddler? Let's say, for illustrative purposes, that the toddler was actually *theirs* (because we all know that toddlers aren't nearly the horror show for other people as they are for their own parents). And maybe, just to make it a bit easier for the students, all they had to do was make the toddler take a nap. *If the toddler sleeps, you get an A. If the toddler trashes his room, takes off his diaper, throws every Matchbox car he owns on the top bunk of his bed, and you find him forty-five minutes later army-crawling down the hallway with his baby sister's pacifier hanging out of his mouth, you Fail.*

Oh, the F's I would have given out.

Chapter 5
No Shirt, No Shoes, No Shame

As I write this, I'm sitting in my driveway in full view of my neighbors. I hear lawnmowers droning in the background, dogs barking, children laughing as they chase each other from the bus stop to their respective homes. All is peaceful and idyllic and being conducted in full accordance with the Homeowners Association bylaws.

I live in the sort of neighborhood where lawns are kept tidy and mowed on a regular basis (except ours), cars are washed (except mine), dogs hang out behind ornate, wrought iron fences (except Ollie, who has a designated radius over which he reigns supreme—as far as his chain can reach), and children are fully clothed when they run around outside (except, you guessed it, mine).

Rollie prefers to have as little clothing on as possible. Regardless of occasion, ambient temperature, time of day, etc., if he had his druthers, Rollie would spend his day jaybird naked (except for footwear, which would vacillate

between a pair of foam-soled flip-flops or a pair of green plastic galoshes). But because he's not yet potty trained, I usually insist that he wear a diaper at the very least as he prances around in his shoes.

So right now he's sporting a swim diaper, because I have also dragged his wading pool into the driveway and am filling it so my son can come up with all sorts of water activities—something two-year-olds are crazy-good at. No telling how many homeowner association rules we are violating just by being outside. I in my camping chair, laptop balanced on my knees, a koozie with a can of diet root beer in one hand, cut-offs, flip-flops, no make-up, watching Rollie determinedly fill an old soap dispenser with water and waddle over to our overgrown flowerbeds so he can squirt their thirsty roots with the sudsy mixture. Elsa is out here splashing around, too, but we'll get to her in a minute.

As I sit, observing the happy activities of my children, I realize a simple truth: White Trash is onto something. Truly. The things my children and I are currently engaging in, White Trash has been doing for *years*. If White Trash had a motto, it would be something like, *why buy something when you can make a perfectly good replica for free?* This would read differently if actual White Trash thought it up, but you get the idea.

Another motto might be: Choose the Path of Least Resistance (again, worded differently). It's aaaall about convenience as far as White Trash is concerned. It's so much easier to just let a child walk around in a diaper, especially in the middle of the summer. Cans are the better drinking receptacle than bottles (portability, size, and the fact that they fit snugly inside a koozie), the driveway really is the best place to gather and watch the world pass by, and it's much more cost-effective to buy a chain for your dog than to go and install an entire fence.

And it's easier to stick my daughter in her bathtub inside of the wading pool than it would be for me to crouch down beside the pool and keep one hand on her slippery little body. She's happy as a pig in you-know-what, kicking her legs and waving her arms and grasping for toys as they float past. She can sit up and splash and watch Rollie play from the comfort of her tub seat. And I don't have to lift a freaking finger.

I think having kids awakens our inner White Trash. Seriously. If you go to a Wal-Mart, you're already on the cusp of White Trash-ness, but if you go to a Wal-Mart with your *child*, you just earned yourself a White Trash point. If that child is missing an article of clothing, there's another point. If that child is barefoot, there's another point. If that child is *walking* barefoot, it's a bonus point. I'm sure I've racked up enough points to earn a guest appearance on Jerry Springer, and maybe even get a chair thrown at my head for free.

I'm sure you too have been judged to be far more White Trash than you actually are. Take the Wal-Mart scenario, for example. Sure you're going in there wearing cutoffs and accompanied by a barefoot child, right? But what people *won't* see is that you were in such a hurry to leave the house because you just finished nursing your new baby, and you only have a specific window in which to run errands before that baby is ready to eat again, and you're only going to Wal-Mart because your dear husband decided that he absolutely has to change your oil that night and needs a new oil filter and has directed you to go to Wal-Mart without fail and pick one up, and because you know better than to argue with your husband on the subject of auto care, you oblige and gather up the troops to make the excursion, but in your haste you neglected to shod your eldest, which explains his lack of footwear.

And then once you arrive at your destination, you realize that your son has spilled his entire box of chocolate milk on his shorts (or his diaper exploded is another legitimate excuse) and you brought the diaper bag with the extra diapers, shirts, wipes, bibs, snacks, every conceivable accessory for any child under three, but dag-nabbit, you failed to pack your son an extra pair of shorts. Good thing you're at Wal-Mart! You can get shorts, shoes, *and* an oil filter.

Hell, you can even pick up a few groceries while you're at it.

So you're going through the store with two very young children, one of which is basically naked from the waist down, and you run into someone you know. Yeah, it looks bad. Depending on how well you know the person, and how judgmental that person may be, you either explain why you're laden with semi-nude children in the middle of the automotive aisle, your self-deprecating humor begging for you to be forgiven, or, if you're like me, you duck behind a display of beach balls and pray your acquaintance passes by without a second glance.

On the Trash-o-Meter, you're hovering somewhere around a seven. Because your child's feet may be exposed, but by God, at least they aren't dirty. And maybe at a weak moment you purchase a Mountain Dew from the checkout cooler, but at least it's not in a can and about to double as an ashtray. See? You have standards.

My point is, don't be afraid to embrace your inner White Trash. I'm telling you, they have it all figured out. The path of least resistance, the easiest way through.

It's easier to get a wading pool than to pile children and the proper accoutrement into the car and drive to an alternative body of water, one where you'd likely have to keep a much closer eye on them instead of letting them kick around in a few inches of floating grass-clippings and plastic pool toys. It's easier to let a kid loose in just a diaper than to go through the hassle of arguing over what shirt, shorts, hat, socks, jacket to wear, and then wrestling that kid into an outfit that comes close to matching. It's easier to repair broken toys with duct tape and thumbtacks than to go out and search for an appropriate spare part or, heaven forbid, buy another one intact. It's easier to cut your child's hair on only the rarest of occasions, say your own wedding, and when you do, only the front of it, letting the back get long and luxurious. It's easier to bathe a child with baby wipes and condensation from your beer can instead of in the tub. Or just not bathe them at all—that's the easiest yet.

Okay, so maybe I'm an imposter. Maybe I still have much to learn about being White Trash. Maybe I've even offended actual White Trash with my ignorance about what being White Trash really entails. All I can say is, I'm still a big fan of letting children play in the driveway. If you're lucky enough to live near a relatively calm street, and have a driveway at least a car-length long, I say, let 'em loose. Build up an arsenal of sidewalk chalk, a few wheeled toys, a wading pool (with a tub inside for the really little ones), assorted bubbles, then pull out your lawn chair, crank up the radio, crack open a beer, and watch the fun. White Trash Style.

Chapter 6
Why 'Because I Said So' Is A Perfectly Acceptable Reason

Sometimes I imagine my brain as a series of filing cabinets. Inside each cabinet are all sorts of things—ideas, song lyrics, memories—filed away to be accessed whenever I need them. Only I don't have a very organized filing system. I'm often digging through piles and piles of useless information (like my memory of the outfit I wore to my seventh grade semi-formal in minute detail, from the ill-fitting, hand-me-down, peach-colored strapless dress to the ill-fitting, hand-me-down, Sam & Libby flats) before I can access the more important stuff (like how to change the television input to DVD so my son can watch *Cars* for the eighty-fifth time).

So anyway, one such file drawer is labeled *Things I'll Never Do When I Have Children*. Inside are little scraps of paper upon which I have written down lines like, *give my child a spit-shine, let him wander the house eating lollipops, take him to Wal-Mart barefoot (him, not me)*. You know, stuff I'd come up with over the years based on my own childhood experiences, or things I've observed other people doing or allowing their children to do that made me cringe. Whenever I

Cow Physics

saw a parent yelling at her child to be quiet, or bribing him to stop whining, or ignoring him when the kid *was* whining, I'd jot down the instance on a mental scrap of paper and stick it in the drawer.

You're laughing already, aren't you?

The other day I grabbed Rollie by the arm. Hard. I didn't leave little finger marks on the flesh (though I almost wished I had…to serve as a reminder not to try to run away from Mommy when she's trying to change you out of wet clothes and into dry ones so we can leave the hundred-degree poolside heat and get everyone into the car before they all spontaneously combust), but I still manhandled him more roughly than I really wanted to. Especially in public, in front of friends, children, strangers, God, etc.

I always swore I would never grab my child by the arm and yank him. I think I filed that little scrap away after watching *The Shining*. It's a mundane detail, really, but Mr. Torrance sends his son to the hospital for dislocating his shoulder with such a yank. Not that I'm now worried Rollie's gonna start talking to his finger and having visions of blood spill down our hallway, but still, the last thing I want to do is send my child to the ER. Scare him a little, maybe, get the point across, absolutely, but certainly not *hurt* him.

That's not the first promise I've broken. Another one of my mother's favorite lines is, *Because I said so*. My mother was no doubt at her wits' end after explaining every nuance of every rule for the past ten years to the four children that preceded me. By the time I rolled around, shooting off my mouth and demanding explanations to everything, she'd had ENOUGH and therefore came up with the catchall, the umbrella reason for every question I could possibly hurl out (probably with an extra helping of sass).

Because I said so. That was the answer I got. Pretty unsatisfactory, even to an eight-year-old. *Especially* to an eight-year-old.

Being a mother myself now, my eyes, as they say, have been opened.

Now I get it. Now I understand why I heard *Because I said so* more often than *The Cosby Show* theme song. If my mother had to give an explanation to every kid who asked for one, she'd *still* be giving lectures. *Because I said so* was invented to salvage what little sanity parents still have.

As of this chapter, my son hasn't even begun the whole 'why' phase (although toward the end of the manuscript he *did* start asking 'why' pretty much every other second…see Chapter 21, The Quick And…The Not-So-Quick). His questioning is still in the 'what's that' phase. Or 'where'd such-and-such go?' Like, when we're driving past a cow, and the cow is no longer in our field of vision, he'll want to know where it went. Which, I have found, is a fairly difficult thing to explain. The cow doesn't really *go* anywhere, we're the ones who're moving, and can no longer see said cow. The cow is behind us now, still there, eating grass and flatulating and doing whatever else it is that cows do these days ("what's he doing" is another favorite question of Rollie's, although it's usually in reference to something that's not really *doing* anything…a leaf, a dead lizard, a fire hydrant…).

But I know soon I will put the phrase *Because I said so* to good use. And really, it's not the worst thing in the world you can tell a preschooler. They need to learn respect. And they don't need an explanation for every little thing. They could ask *why* all the live-long day, breaking your answers down to the atomic level, but all that will do is leave you exhausted and incapable of forming any more words once your children have gone to bed—you will have far exceeded your verbal quota for the day. *Because I said so* is a nice substitute for an actual explanation, and can work in every situation. Sit down in your chair. Eat your vegetables. Don't stick your hand in the toilet. (Side note—I have also found the phrase *Because it's yucky* to work in many, many situations. I think this phrase will come in handy more for boys than girls, but don't hesitate to use it as often as is appropriate. Every five minutes is probably a safe bet.)

Now, there will be times when *Because I said so* will lose its effectiveness.

A time when your child will go ahead and do whatever it is you've asked him not to do, or vice versa, just to see if he can. Just to see if your words carry some sort of magic powers that will render him immobile, turn him to salt or stone or any other substance. And that's when you have to start threatening.

I've had to get pretty creative with my threats. It's like constantly finding the Achilles Heel, which changes daily. Sometimes it's an Achilles Finger, an Achilles Clavicle, an Achilles Left Buttock:

Rollie, pick up that ball right now or you can't play baseball anymore.

Rollie, turn off your light or you don't get a popsicle.

Rollie, get your feet off your sister or I'll tie your ankles together.

One threat I've found quite effective is threatening to leave the house without him. Of course, I have no intention of doing so, but as long as *he* doesn't know this, I am safe to use this threat as much as possible. Usually it only comes in handy when I'm scrambling to get out of the house, and Rollie is purposefully ignoring my pleas for him to hurry, to put on his shoes, to stop trying to drag his dirty tricycle across my newly vacuumed carpet. You know, typical two-year-old crap.

All I have to say is "I'm leaving without you," and then actually make like I'm going to, and he'll come running. Of course, the day will come when he'll call my bluff and go on dragging his dirty tricycle, in which case I may have to actually get into the car, back out of the driveway and make it all the way to say, Atlanta, before he bursts into tears and runs after me, but I'll drive over that bridge without him when I come to it.

Threatening to take something away also works well, just make sure you're willing and able to do it. I've had to stop myself from threatening to throw out Rollie's toys if he didn't pick them up, just because I really can't imagine bagging up all his stuff and tossing it in the garbage. What a waste of money. Plus, throwing away his toys would be more of a punishment on me than him.

Sometimes employing the old 'count to three' method still works. I started using this on Rollie before he turned two, and I think it works because the first time I did it, I got all the way to three and ended up giving him a swat on his diapered bottom. He instantly fell to pieces (and I instantly felt terrible for spanking him), but since I've been using this method I've only gotten to 'three' one other time. And when I did say 'three,' Rollie fell into such a panic that I didn't have to swat him—he'd mentally beaten himself up with the fear that I was about to. Sometimes the anticipation is worse than the punishment.

I can attest to that. When we were kids, my siblings and I were a pretty obedient bunch. But if we misbehaved, our father spanked us. If we misbehaved en route somewhere, our father let us know that we were going to *get* a spanking when we got home. Sometimes this would mean sitting through an entire church service, coffee hour and forty-five-minute car ride back home, during which we would think about nothing but the fact that we were going to get a spanking at home, and hope like hell our father would forget. He never did. Even if we were somewhere far away, like Virginia, and acted up, our father vowed to spank us when we got home, thereby making the six-hour drive to New Jersey quite miserable. Like a long, drawn-out last meal on death row.

And so, the one-two-three method seems to work for us now. And lose-a-toy. And I'm-leaving-without-you. Feel free to combine any and all of these in any order you find fitting.

Because I said so.

Chapter 7
I Do Anal

    I read somewhere that kids thrive on schedules, and mothers should strive to make them. I used to think that applied only to Alpha Moms, those super uptight, anal-retentive mothers who are always dashing off to ballet recitals, soccer matches, piano lessons, putting their children down for naps precisely at one-forty, having delicious, eye-catchingly presented meals on the dinner table by 6 p.m. Schedules weren't for me, nor were they for my children, who I vowed would be as laid-back and cool as I was.

    But really, whoever wrote that schedule bit knew what she was talking about. Kids do thrive on them. Or maybe a more accurate way to put it is, they fall apart at the freaking seams if they *have* a schedule and you do something, anything, that slightly offsets it. It isn't pretty.

    But what's even less pretty is what happens to *Mommy* when someone messes with that schedule. Especially if that someone happens to be Daddy.

    Now, don't get me wrong. I love my husband (haha…doesn't sound

so obvious when used in that context, does it?). He is such a good dad. Maybe that's the problem. Monday through Friday, Mom runs the show. Mom gets breakfast, gets clothes put on, gets the teeth brushed, the beds made, the butts wiped, the shoes laced, the juice flowing, the snacks coming. Mom is the playmate, the mediator, the teacher, the worker of the TV remotes.

But Saturday morning....dah dah dah DAAAH! It's Daddy Day! A day of joy, of fun, of thumbing your nose at the rules, and making forts out of the couch cushions Mommy spends five days a week trying to keep clean and straight.

I'm not proud to admit this, but sometimes when I see my husband doing something ridiculously fun for our son, like setting up the garden hose to cascade a delightfully refreshing stream of water onto him as he pedals around on his tricycle, or kicking a soccer ball around the dining room table for literally 45 minutes with Rollie, I cringe. I have to bite my tongue from voicing my concern that my husband is having too much fun with Rollie. Why? What's the matter with me? What kind of fun-crushing bitch am I to actually worry that my son and his father are having an absolute blast?

Because I will be burdened with the impossible task of replicating this fun. This new game, whether it be Dino-Daddy or Let's Run Around The House From The Pretend Snake Coming To Get Us, is expected to be worked into the daily rotation of laundry or dishes or balancing the checkbook. And while I'd *rather* be playing with Rollie, constructing his train set or reading him stories, the household chores ain't gonna do themselves. And God forbid I leave those tasks unfinished until naptime. When the planets align and the tides cease and my children actually agree to sleep at the same time, I'll be damned if I'm gonna use those precious, precious minutes to Swiffer the floor. Hell no. When else am I gonna write, check my email, Facebook, Twitter, and peruse Craig's List without interruption?

That's what naps are for. That's what schedules are for. And pity the fool who dares screw with Mommy's schedule.

It's not that I *want* to be anal. It just sort of happened, like the stretch marks and the spider veins. I've given birth to an anal streak (ew, that sounded really disgusting).

Maybe it's a survival skill. If I weren't anal, my kids would be animals, raised by wolves, running wild without clothes or food or manners (well, without food anyway). I think part of being a mom is being a somewhat strict taskmaster, with all the ruler-tapping, head-smacking discipline of a nun-run Catholic school. It's not fun. I've discovered that I don't like implementing rules, enforcing them, and doling out the discipline when the rules are broken. It's a drag, really. But it's totally necessary.

Sometimes, however, the anal roles are reversed. Like at the grocery store. My husband came shopping with us recently to our neighborhood store. I'm not sure who he wanted to kill more by the end of the trip, Rollie or me. I let Rollie walk instead of making him ride in the cart. We cruise by the bakery so he can get a free cookie (yes, my store actually has a punch card for this—once Rollie has gotten ten free cookies his name goes into a drawing for a really big free cookie—how cool is that?), we go by the deli and get free slices of cheese and turkey, we go by the lobster tank and check those out. Rollie sometimes brings a little Matchbox car with him to run along the dairy case. It's a nice little trip, usually just Rollie, Elsa and me, and things go pretty smoothly (or not—see Chapter 15, The Incredible Journey—To The Grocery Store).

Bring Daddy into the picture, and things just get crazy. Jeff lunges after our son if Rollie gets anywhere beyond a two-foot radius of the cart. And because Jeff was a grocery stock boy in high school, he cringes if Rollie messes with a display of canned tuna or knocks over a stack of cereal boxes—he knows what a pain in the ass it is to align items on a grocery shelf (although if you ask me, keeping a two-year-old entertained at the grocery store is an even bigger pain in the ass).

At one point during our family grocery store trip, Jeff turned to me and said, "So this is what you let him do?"

Ah, I bet those were some poor husband's last words.

All I could do was shake my head. Anything I would have said in response to this comment would have come out as A.) Scathing, B.) Annoyed, or C.) Defensive:

A.) Yes, I let him run around like a lunatic because I enjoy watching other people click their tongues and frown in disapproval—it reaffirms my fear that I am a bad mother.

B.) Yes, but let me know if you have a better option that keeps him from whining and totally distracting me so that I forget to buy you deodorant.

C.) Oh, shut up.

So yeah, I'm not the only one who can be anal around here. Unfortunately, I'm not into the kind of anal my husband would like. But alas, I digress....

Chapter 8
Naptime (aka: Let's See How Many Facebook Walls I Can Write On Before They Wake Up)

Here's a scenario for you…tell me if it sounds familiar:

The clock on my laptop reads 12:42 p.m. One of my children is sleeping peacefully in her crib, quiet and plump as a little cherub. The room breathes with each sweet exhale, the soft clicks of her mouth as she sucks her pacifier are the only sounds in the muted afternoon light that filters through the cracks of her drawn window shades. All is calm, subdued and sleepy.

In my son's room…not so much. A bang emits from behind his door (as long as a shriek doesn't follow, I don't bother investigating). He's supposed to be taking a nap, but napping doesn't interest him right now. Not as much as trying to see how many toy cars he can launch across his windowsill and into his garbage can before Mom comes in and spoils the fun.

Nap time. Ah yes, that tranquil, lethargic two hours in the afternoon when I don't hear any fussing, whining, requests for juice, Wubzy, a bite of whatever I might be enjoying. The only time when I don't hear a peep from my children and instantly suspect they're either engaged in something totally illegal, or they're pooping. (Of course, this only happens if you can get your child to actually *take* a nap.)

I have a fun activity for you: Barge into the middle of your child playing with something—dolls, cars, cat food, whatever—and announce the dreaded, seven letter word. Naptime. Do it and see what happens. I'll wait...

How'd it go? Not so great, huh? Suggesting that my son take a nap is like asking him to take every toy in his room, put them in a garbage bag and smash them to bits with a sledge hammer. Never mind that he's miserable, dragging himself from room to room in my wake, whining for a movie he doesn't like or a cup of juice he doesn't want or a toy I don't think he even has anymore. It's torture. For me. It takes everything in my power not to shut him out of my room, lie down on my bed, turn the volume up on VH1 and watch *I Love The 80's* for the tenth time, reminiscing about when I was nine and had no children to hear whimpering in the background and banging on my bedroom door.

Here's another fun activity: Put a child who swears up and down he's not tired into his room and hold the bedroom door shut. Stand in the hallway with your hand on the knob, feel the pull and twist from the other side as a toddler exerts every ounce of force he has to free himself from naptime prison. Try not to laugh as you do this—your child cannot know that you are still within earshot. He must believe that the door is somehow being held in place by some magical, unseen being, Ruler of the Nap Dimension, and no amount of pulling and banging on his side of the door will cause said door to open, thus releasing him from his cell. Then stand there and listen. You will hear some of the funniest stuff you've ever heard in your life.

The other day I tried this activity and heard all sorts of things. My son recited *Brown Bear, Brown Bear*, a Bible story and *Goodnight Moon*, adding the same commentary I do when I read those stories to him. Then I heard him talking to his Elmo doll, telling him not to be afraid, it was only naptime and to lie down under his covers. Then I heard a series of crashes and bangs, which I identified as him pulling out his wooden puzzles and scattering the pieces around his room. Then I heard him asking himself where the various pieces went, and correcting himself if he put a piece in the wrong spot.

Then I heard him speak sharply to his Elmo doll, whom I could only assume had gotten out of bed.

"Get in bed, Elmo," Rollie said. "It's naptime. You may not get up until you take a nap."

I waited, lips pressed together to keep from laughing out loud.

"Naughty, Elmo. You're in time out." I heard the closet door slide open and then a thud as my son threw Elmo to the floor, which activated him to start singing the *Sesame Street* theme song in his annoying, muffled little voice.

"No talking, Elmo, you're in time out." The closet door rumbled shut, silencing Elmo.

I heard clattering, then my son mumbling that he couldn't find his favorite car. Then he started singing the alphabet off-key, ending the song with a rousing "Yay," which would normally be my part. He made airplane noises, car noises, animal noises, and I pictured him playing with the respective toys, constantly moving, anything to keep from succumbing to exhaustion (and I knew he was exhausted—he'd been up since 5 a.m. and hadn't napped the day before—the toddler equivalent to a 3-day coke binge).

Finally I opened the door. Rollie stood there in a t-shirt and diaper, his pants cast aside like a rumpled prom dress. He clutched a Matchbox airplane in one hand and his beloved elephant blankie in the other. On the floor, lined up like tiny Rockettes, were dozens of animal figurines. I burst out laughing. I couldn't help it. It must have taken him so much time and concentration to get his animals arranged so perfectly—their tiny hooves make it difficult for them to stand on the carpet. Yet there they all were, one after another, staring out at me but not ratting out their creator.

"Look, Mamma," Rollie said, pointing at his handiwork.

"I see," I said, trying not to make it obvious how funny I found the scene.

"Do you want to play with me?" he asked innocently, as if I'd merely barged in on him doing something virtuous, like cleaning his room.

"I would love to play with you," I said, "after you take a nap."

I said this because I'd always read that just about anything can sound appealing to a kid if you put a positive spin on it.

Apparently no one told Rollie this. Because as soon as I said it, he started doing the Toddler Twist, which is flailing his arms, stomping his feet and flopping his head around like he's having a seizure.

"I don't want to take a nap," he shouted.

"I know, honey, but if you don't take a nap, you won't feel well later."

"I don't *want* to take a nap."

"You have to take a nap." I didn't bother adding that this was Mommy's Sacred Time, between the hours of 2 and 4 p.m., when she can get online and write or read or perhaps even take a nap herself because she's exhausted from waking up every ninety minutes to attend to one or both children. Such an explanation would fall on deaf ears. I know *I* certainly couldn't appreciate Mommy's Sacred Time when I was a kid. I absolutely *despised* naptime. My mother would usher me into my room right at 2, and on the other side of the wall I could hear the theme song to *As The World Turns* as she settled in to watch her soap operas while I lay in my bed and seethed. To this day, I feel queasy when I hear that song.

I'm sure I'm breaking dozens of cardinal rules by even mentioning this, but sometimes I get tired of pleading with my son to take a nap. Sometimes I just give in. Which is probably how naptime has escalated into such a production. Unless he falls asleep in the car, Rollie simply won't lie down in his bed and take a nap when asked. So when this happens, when I finally give up and let the lion out of his cage, I recruit the help of the best babysitter I've ever found. Mr. Television.

I like to think that I am not a television statistic. You ever hear those surveys where one hundred parents of pre-school kids are asked how many hours of TV a day their children watch? Apparently one hour is the maximum for kids Rollie's age. One Hour. Good Lord, Rollie's reached that quota pretty much before I've had my first cup of coffee. At least the programs he likes are somewhat educational. That's what that nice lady says at the beginning of each show, anyway (if you have Nick Jr., you know what I'm talking about). I let him watch *Lazy Town* because hey, it teaches children about good health habits, and not to discriminate against people with big chins and funny, Icelandic accents. And he watches *Ni-Hao, Kai-Lan* to learn about Chinese Language and Culture, and to help decimate Chinese stereotypes (even though the only adult on the show is Kai-Lan's wise old grandfather. And one of the characters is obsessed with panda bears.) So, you know…it's not like he's watching *total* crap.

But on days he doesn't take a nap, I swear it's like he's in front of the TV all day long. Which would be my fault, right? I should be engaging him during his waking hours (he *is* the first born, after all—see Chapter 2 for a refresher course). In my defense, I did read somewhere that a person uses even less brain power when watching TV than sleeping. So really, he's getting more rest when he *doesn't* nap, right? He's almost comatose, right? Naptime, shmaptime, give me a TV set when 2 o'clock rolls around. I'll have the most well-rested, healthy, culturally aware kid on the block.

Chapter 9
Step Away From The Scissors

I would like to address something here that is a bit difficult to bring up. Mainly because I can totally and completely sympathize with anyone out there who's found themselves guilty of this particular crime. I've been there. I know what it's like, and I know how easily this can happen. But I must say this for all moms, young and old, no matter how many or what age your children are. Please listen closely:

Don't cut your hair. Don't wear sweatpants in the daytime. Don't let your bikini line start growing down your inner thighs. Don't wear stained clothing.

Don't stop caring.

I say this having been to the abyss—having looked into the darkened Pit of Aesthetic Apathy and seen how unattractive it is. Literally. It wears high-waisted Mom-jeans. It can't be bothered with make-up. It doesn't shave. And it doesn't care.

Okay, let's see a show of hands right now—everyone whose husband has uttered the phrase at least once during your marriage, *You're pretty no matter what*. It's a nice sentiment, it's meant to make you feel better and ignore the fact that you put on fifty pounds during pregnancy and your baby only weighed in at eight-point-five. Or that you've accumulated a multitude of 'comfortable' jeans, jeans whose waistlines have started to creep up and grow larger, thereby making an ass that would appear normal in regular clothes now look so large it blocks your peripheral vision. Or that you can't remember the last time you tweezed your eyebrows—you're not even sure where your tweezers *are*—and you're starting to take on an alarming resemblance to Burt on *Sesame Street*.

I hate to point out the obvious, but we've changed. Our current bodies are not the taut, firm, stretch-mark-free figures we had in our teens and twenties. We have wrinkles (or *fine lines*, although I am not fine with any lines on my face, thank you), gray hairs, and spider veins. We've torn in places where no woman should ever even *hear* the word tear in reference to. We've successfully birthed or adopted beautiful children we'd do anything for, protect from anything, children we love more than we thought it was possible to love another human being.

I know that society puts entirely too much emphasis on women's appearance, and that there's a double standard and everyone should be comfortable in their own skin and blah blah blah. I'm fine with all that. I get it. But still…I don't want to look like the beaten-down, sleep-deprived, eternally frazzled Mom that currently occupies my thirty-one-year-old body. I don't want to look like I have given up.

One of the first things women do shortly after giving birth is cut their hair. I did it. After Rollie turned one, I decided that I didn't like long hair anymore. I chopped it off. And I'll admit, it was easier. And it didn't look bad…at first. It looked *"cute." I* looked cute, like a puppy, or an Easter dress.

But I didn't feel right in short hair. Somehow I felt less…feminine. Less sexy. To get over this vague feeling of androgyny, I told myself that it didn't matter. I wasn't *supposed* to be sexy anymore. I was a mom now, and moms weren't sexy—we were maternal, nurturing, comfort food. We were the Macaroni and Cheese of the female species. Everyone likes a little Mac and Cheese, right?

Well…husbands don't like Mac and Cheese. Okay, let me rephrase… husbands don't like Mac and Cheese *every night for dinner*. Sometimes husbands like steak, or stew, or chicken potpie. In many respects, they're simple creatures, husbands, but they don't want to feel cheated. They married a woman they were attracted to. Yes, they were. You know that whole thing about men being visual creatures? So true.

And dammit, they still *want* to find you attractive. Don't you still want to be attracted to them? How would you like it if your husband started walking around in his tighties, let his hair grow long, didn't trim errant nose hairs (okay, some men are beyond hope when it comes to personal grooming), did absolutely nothing to make himself more appealing to you? Or say you're not as interested in looks, but let's say your previously intelligent, able-bodied husband came home from work day after day, parked himself on the couch and watched Jackass marathons well into the night, threw beer cans directly onto the floor, and grunted in response to anything you said. Ew. That's not macaroni and cheese, that's like, cigarette butts and warm, flat beer.

So I'm just sayin'. Don't let yourself go. Don't stop trying. We are not yesterday's moms. We're not doomed to be dowdy and frumpy and sentenced to a life of bad hair and big-butted jeans. Go get a pedicure, a hot pair of panties, a sexy little shirt. Just put down the scissors and back slowly out of the room.

Chapter 10
Are Children No Longer Starving In China?

I'm a pretty laid-back mom. My son doesn't do a whole lot that really gets under my skin. Even when he unraveled an entire roll of toilet paper or pulled every conceivable hygiene product from beneath my bathroom sink or even when he started helping himself to kibble from our dog's bowl—none of those things made me want to tear out chunks of my own hair.

But sit my kid down at the dinner table with me, and after about ten minutes I'm ready to grab that fish stick (or whatever other food he's toying with instead of eating) and cram it into that angelic, condiment-covered face.

When he was still a baby, Rollie was a garbage disposal, eating pretty much anything we put on his highchair tray. But sometime between his first and second birthdays, he's become quite the dinnertime challenge. We've tried all sorts of creative tactics to get him to willingly eat. For a while we tried to distract him with a TV show while we'd smuggle food into his gaping mouth and remind him to make like a train and chew-chew-chew. When that

Mommy's Food Pyramid

stopped working, we'd attempt to make him laugh, practically pulling muscles as we contorted our faces into whatever theatrical expressions would elicit a chuckle from our son, during which the one who wasn't the designated jester would quickly stuff a morsel in his mouth. But that too lost its charm—the routine became exhausting for us, and as he grew older, the stunts we needed to perform became more complex. At that rate, we'd have to be shooting ourselves out of a cannon by the time Rollie turned five.

And so for a time, every bite of dinner was the result of a long, calculated bargain.

>Me: Have some broccoli, Rollie.
>
>Rollie: Juice.
>
>Me: Take a bite first.
>
>Rollie: Juice please.
>
>Me (*broccoli-laden fork poised in front of his face*): First take a bite.
>
>Rollie: I want juice.
>
>Me: You aren't getting any juice until you take a bite of this broccoli.
>
>*Rollie opens his mouth, then shuts it again as the offending broccoli approaches.*
>
>Me: Rollie, please take this one bite and then you can have your juice.
>
>Rollie: It's too big.
>
>Me: No it's not, you can do it, just this one bite.
>
>Rollie: No, it's too big.
>
>Me (*after pruning the broccoli down to the size of a raisin*): Here, that's not too big. Now eat it.
>
>*Rollie opens his mouth and leans in for the bite. My shoulders relax as a smug*

sense of accomplishment washes over me. Then he shuts his mouth again.

Rollie: It's too hot.

Me: There's no way it's too hot, Rol. It's been sitting out for ten minutes.

Rollie: It's too cold.

Me: Well, I'm not heating it up—you should have eaten it ten minutes ago. Now take a bite.

Rollie: It's yucky.

Me (*sighing so heavily the force of it blows his napkin to the floor*): Rollie, you ate broccoli just the other day and you loved it. You ate every bite of it and asked for more. You smiled and made yummy noises and laughed because you liked it so much. Now you are going to eat this bite of broccoli and you're going to eat it NOW.

Rollie: Juice.

This will go on for several more rounds until finally I'll either threaten him with never giving him another drop of juice so long as we both shall live, or my husband will sense that I'm about to have a serious meltdown, and he'll intervene, all fresh-faced and different-approachied, making airplane noises with Rollie's fork, leaving me to retreat to the fridge for a much-needed adult beverage.

What I don't understand is why my son's resistance to ingest anything that isn't in the shape of a goldfish or a hue not found in nature bothers me so much. He's big for a two-year-old, energetic and fast. He never complains that he's hungry, he's hardly ever sick. He's obviously getting his nutrients from somewhere. I don't get it. Does he wait until everyone is sleeping, then raid the fridge, dining on heaps of vegetables and fruit, grains and lean meats, covering the entire food pyramid each night so he can subsist on grapes and air during the day? Or is he more like a camel, storing vitamins and minerals somewhere on his person, feeding off of them slowly through self-induced famine?

All day long I go through a mental checklist of everything that's passed my son's lips, tallying up the calories, fats, proteins, vitamins, trying to determine if he needs to have applesauce for dessert (to round out his servings of fruits), of if he should have frozen yogurt instead (for calcium and protein). I expend more energy obsessing over his menu than I do actually preparing him anything.

Perhaps my son's lack of appetite is my fault. Maybe I'm too accommodating. If he turns up his little button nose at spaghetti, I dig around for something I think he'll accept. He seems to know this—he has no fear that he'll starve if he refuses the first thing set before him. Maybe I should instill a little fear in him. Maybe the next time he looks at me like he's about to call child protective services because I served him such slop, I should simply remove his plate and tell him he's not getting anything. That'll teach him. Until he learns how to dial the phone and DCF comes knocking.

I know in about ten years, I'll be wondering if my son will ever *stop* eating. I grew up with brothers. When a house contains at least one growing boy, the rate at which food disappears is staggering, like an army of siafu ants has descended upon the house, turning a once-stocked pantry into a wasteland of empty boxes, shredded bags, and jars containing nothing but dregs. Don't stand still too long in a kitchen with a couple of ravenous teenage boys—you may end up a carcass, your bones picked clean.

To me, the distant promise of a monstrous grocery bill and being eaten out of house and home is a light at the end of a tunnel. Until then, I am resigned to hover over my son, spooning food into his mouth while the TV distracts him, fretting about him meeting his caloric needs, and scouring the grocery store for food I can prepare quickly—there's no point in spending more than 5 minutes on a meal that will take him only a few seconds to decide he'd rather fling across the kitchen than eat.

I long for the day when my brain can be preoccupied with other things, like trying to decide what *I* want for dinner. Although by the time I actually eat, all I want is something simple, like wine. Because unlike my son, I am *not* a growing boy, and alcohol is enough of a food pyramid for me.

Chapter 11
Playdate Etiquette (aka: Let's Vacuum The House In A Full-On Sprint Ten Minutes Before The Doorbell Rings—It's Great Cardio)

If you've had kids for any amount of time, you've probably either been to (or if you've gone through a bout of temporary insanity, decided to host) a playdate.

When they don't take place at your own house, playdates are great. I drag Rollie and Elsa to them all the time. It's really an excuse for my kids to play with toys I didn't have to buy, while I eat food I didn't have to prepare and drink coffee I didn't have to make. And I get to interact with people whose favorite word isn't 'poopy.' I stretch my vocabulary muscles and hold conversations that don't necessarily include calling threats across the house or bargaining with someone to take one more bite or get himself dressed (unless you are the host…which you'll read about shortly). If you're lucky enough to have a few

Playdates - Better Without Glasses

friends with kids the same age as yours, one of the best favors you can do for your own sanity is get together with them once in a while. Get out of your house. As fast as you can.

The only downside of having a playdate group is that you will inevitably have to *host* a playdate. I mean, unless you can come up with a fantastical excuse as to why you couldn't possibly have ten kids who aren't yours traipsing about your house. I'm still trying to come up with one that's believable. *I'm getting new carpeting put in* or *I just painted all the rooms* can only take you so far. Eventually you will have to give in and host one your damn self.

The best kind of playdate you can host is one where everyone is outside. These seem to be the least destructive, and yield the best naps afterwards. I am at an advantage, living in Florida, because outdoor playdates are possible almost year-round. In fact, the hotter the better, because hot playdates tend to produce the most physically exhausted children in the shortest amount of time. As long as they don't get heat stroke, you should be fine.

Sometimes, however, outdoor playdates aren't an option. And when the time comes for you to host an indoor playdate, my best advice to you is: Try not to pay too much attention to anything. If you wear contacts, don't bother putting them in; if you have glasses, don't wear them. You don't want to see the havoc that is being wreaked on your house. Make sure your children aren't watching, either. They are just as uncomfortable with the situation as you are… maybe more so. They don't want to see their beloved train set scattered around the family room like so many playing cards. They don't want to share anything with anyone, and they won't be shy about making their trepidation known. Loud and clear.

I usually try to make my house look less like a home to several farm animals and more like a place where people might actually want to hang out, and possibly even let their precious children play. Luckily I have been blessed with a circle of non-judgmental friends. They don't care that I have a layer of dust thick enough to be called accumulation on my TV, that my coffee mugs don't match, or that my carpet has more stains than Jackson Pollock's smock. Still, ten minutes before guests arrive I am inevitably tearing around the house, vacuuming, wiping surfaces (see Chapter 19, Guide To Half-Assed Cleaning), making muffins (not from scratch, mind you...I'm not *that* sick), dragging toys out of closets and shoving everything else *into* closets and hoping like hell that no one actually *opens* a closet. Nothing like squeezing in some good cardio before your house turns into Romper Room.

One thing about having a bunch of kids over to your house—don't expect to be able to carry on any semblance of conversation with any of your guests. Oh sure, you can try to string a coherent sentence together here and there, but be prepared for interruptions (honey, please don't throw that at the fireplace) distractions (where did I just set that mug of coffee for so-and-so?) and moments of pure terror (oh my God, so-and-so's kid has figured out how to work my remote and my husband's skin flick is now playing on our big-screen TV).

Once the playdate is over and everyone goes home, you will feel hung over. Your nerves are shot, your mouth is dry, and you're probably a bit shaky from all the excitement. You owe it to yourself to take the rest of the day off. Relax. Have a drink. Plop your children in front of the TV and put your feet up. Engage in something mindless—surf the Net or read a stupid magazine. You need about six-to-eight weeks to recover before you even *think* about having people over again.

And next time you do, for God's sake, erase the TiVo'd porn!

Chapter 12
Excuse Me, But Your Nipple Is Showing

Having kids means that they will ultimately embarrass the crap out of you. If you haven't had a mortifying incident yet, don't worry, you will. Spit-up you didn't notice in your hair but everyone else in line at Starbucks can smell from a mile away. A half-eaten lollipop stuck to your ass that you don't find until you've walked the entire mall, upstairs and down, and sat down to devour a slice of pizza.

Or, like me, exposing yourself to the cashier at your local grocery store.

Before children, I was hyper-self-aware. At least once an hour, I checked my appearance out in a mirror or other reflective surface just to make sure my teeth were spinach-free and my hair wasn't sticking out everywhere. I'm not one of those women who always looks polished and made-up by any means, but before kids, I showered daily, brushed my hair and tried to make it out the door with, at the bare minimum, some lip gloss, and in most instances, a bra.

I did all of this because I had time. I didn't have to rush showers because my child was crawling around the bathroom floor and whining because she got stuck behind the toilet, or because I realized mid-shower that my son had consumed three cups of juice and hadn't peed yet, and being in the fledgling stages of potty training was wearing a new pair of big-boy undies. I had plenty of time to give myself a proper pedicure and make sure I was wearing all appropriate undergarments.

During this blissful, child-free era, I saw a commercial with a woman talking about the ease with which she could use whatever product she was pitching, and how nice it was to have one thing in her life that she could count on, as about a dozen kids swarmed around her like piranhas. Then she smirked at the camera and said something like, "I can't even count on taking a *shower* every day." I remember sitting there on the sofa, probably flipping through a magazine or eating or engaging in some other luxurious and leisurely activity that I used to revel in pre-children, and thinking in disbelief, *now why can't this poor woman count on taking a shower every day? Is her life really so hectic that she can't squeeze in five minutes under a spray of water, give the old pits and crotch a little how's-your-father, maybe slather on some Pert and give everything a good rinse before anyone notices her absence and all hell breaks loose?*

How smug and naïve of me. How very smug and very, very naïve.

The other day in the checkout line, I exposed myself to the cashier.

I didn't mean to. Honest. I'm not into that kind of thing (much to my husband's chagrin). And trust me, after nursing two kids and swiftly closing in on thirty-five, the last thing I want everyone at my friendly neighborhood Publix to see is my boob. Maybe my bra-strap, my lower back or in the worst of cases, a little crack, fine. I can deal with that. But really, my boob? And not just my boob—my nipple. My *nipple*. I'm Saint Augustine's version of Janet Jackson.

Before you laugh, know that it could have happened to you. You, too, could have been mistaken for a Girls Gone Wild audition. Moms and Mayhem. I mean, it happened so fast, yet it still replays in my head in painful, high-def slow motion.

There I was, standing in line with my children, waiting to pay for my groceries like a perfectly respectable member of society. Then Rollie told me he wanted to help slide my card—something I started allowing since it was the only way to keep him from destroying the Tic Tac display. I picked him up and held him on my hip, guiding his hand as he ran my card through the machine and punched in my PIN. That day I wore a tank top with one of those built in bras, usually a bonus because since having kids I've found that some days not only do I sometimes skip taking shower, but I've also started taking shortcuts when getting dressed (I'm still waiting for them to come out with jeans that have socks attached to the cuffs, and shorts with built-in underwear).

Unfortunately, holding my darling, thirty-pound-boy on my hip while wearing an only somewhat-supportive tank top and being distracted with making sure he didn't type in the wrong code and lead to my purchase being declined (now wouldn't *that* have been embarrassing?) was not the wisest thing I could have done. Because after completing my transaction, I looked up at the cashier, waiting for the automatic and obligatory *have a nice day*, and perhaps a comment about how simply adorable my son is, I noticed that her eyes weren't meeting mine in a friendly smile. Oh no. Her eyes were instead focused on something else, and they were quite large and round.

And suddenly I had a premonition, a terrible, terrible sense that something awful was about to happen. Had my son left chocolate handprints all over my shirt? Had Elsa wiped a booger on my chest? Was a giant tarantula creeping its way up my torso?

All of those would have been welcome alternatives to what the cashier was actually staring at. Because just then I felt oddly exposed…and a little

Excuse Me...

chilly. I looked down. Yep. There it was. My boob, nipple, areola and all.

Balancing Rollie on my hip had pulled my shirt down at the bottom, causing the neckline to sag, pull, and eventually give up its cargo, revealing it to the poor cashier and anyone else who wanted to take a gander.

"Whoa," I said, dropping my son like a hot, whining potato and adjusting my shirt. "Yikes. Sorry about that."

After the slightest pause, during which I'm sure the cashier was making every attempt to banish the image from her mind, she smiled and shook her head.

"That's okay," she said, like I'd just given her an expired coupon instead of her own personal peepshow. But I could still see the look in her eyes. She was young, possibly in college (*please God don't let me just have flashed a high school girl*), and definitely didn't have kids. I could tell by her face. She looked disbelieving, and a bit…smug. I knew what she was thinking. *God, lady, don't you even notice when your boob is hanging out there for the whole world to see? Shouldn't you be wearing a bra—you have kids for crying out loud. Women your age should be wearing turtlenecks and sweatpants.*

That's what *I* would have been thinking, ten years and two kids ago. That's what I used to think when I saw that commercial with that stinky, shower-skipping lady, or whenever I'd see a harried, frazzled, frumpy-looking mother bustling a flock of children through my checkout line. I'd take one look at the stained shirt, the frizzy hair, the naked face of the woman as she pawed through her purse for coupons and her checkbook as she barked at her kids to stop messing with the Tic Tacs and I'd think, *Kill me if I'm ever that disheveled and un-self-aware.*

Good thing no one ever held me to *that* pact.

Chapter 13
The Octopus And The Butterfly

Remember a while back in the book when I said something about how being a mom can convince you that you're losing your mind? Of course you don't...you're too busy keeping your child from turning a bowl of dog food into a ball-pit for his G.I. Joe—you can't remember what you had for breakfast, let alone something some lady wrote in a book seventy-five pages ago.

Anyway, what I meant was that when you're a mom, you tend to take on multiple personalities. You're still You, in a sense. The fundamentals of who you are, Type A, Type B, Type Why-In-God's-Name-Did-I-Stop-Taking-My-Birth-Control-Pills, are still there. But you've also sort of adopted a few new personas.

And I don't mean that now you're a teacher, a healer, a chef, a chauffeur....I mean, you *are* all those things, but you're also a critic. And apparently a total bee-yatch.

I realized *I'd* become these things the day I watched my husband make a sandwich. I stood beside him at the counter as he lathered his bread with various condiments and piled on the cold cuts. Then he produced a knife and pressed down on the bread, severing the sandwich in two, its contents spilling out onto his plate.

"Wow," I said.

That was it. One word and suddenly I knew what I'd become. The second I said it I started to laugh.

My husband looked up at me, bewildered.

"What's so funny?"

"Nothing," I said. "It's just…I wouldn't have cut my sandwich that way."

"What way?"

"Squishing it down like that." I laughed again. I laughed so hard I couldn't continue. I couldn't tell my husband the awful truth: The woman he'd married ten years ago, the one who could drink him under the table and despised Disney World and watched shows about serial killers, was gone. And in her place was a mommy, a woman who now spends more time interacting with a two-year-old and an infant than any adult. Naturally, I would be quick to notice that my husband's sandwich halves looked gutted and cauterized. I've been reprogrammed to find ways to improve everything, to explain everything, to make everything better for everyone, like I'm some domestic superhero sent to the planet to make sure that sandwich is cut perfectly to maximize the eater's enjoyment. Wonderbread Woman to the rescue!

Admit it. You too used to be fun, carefree and uncritical. But having a kid is like having this cute, onesie-clad little disease ravaging your brain, eating up the important information you used to know—literature, equations, how to make a dirty martini—and replacing it with stuff like the cook time for chicken nuggets, which grocery store has those shopping carts shaped like cars, where your son stashed his favorite Matchbox car (answer: inside his new potty).

What we need to determine is—is all the other stuff gone forever? Are we doomed to watch our significant others slice a sandwich and think about how *we* would have done it and how we can coach him to do it correctly next time? Surely not!

Take my sister Amy. After the birth of her third child, my husband nicknamed Amy "The Octopus." Apparently there is an octopus out there that lays eggs, and after she has done so, she sits around and blows on them. She devotes her entire existence to blowing on her eggs, keeping the current flowing around them just right until they hatch. And as soon as they do, she dies.

Amy wasn't always an octopus. She used to be fun. She used to dance on bars and go hiking and picnicking and she has a Master's degree and has traveled to Europe and Mexico and India. But something happened with that first child, and only got worse with kids two and three. Suddenly she was absent from family gatherings—I mean, she was there, but off in another room, bathing or feeding or soothing someone to sleep, always preoccupied with the general welfare and comfort of three other human beings. She could no longer play the drinking games that she herself had taught us all. She couldn't stay up late for karaoke or poker or Guitar Hero. Not when she knew she'd be awakened several times during the night to find a pacifier or change a diaper, not when she had to be up at 5:30 a.m. to pour the Lucky Charms.

Now her kids are older and somewhat self-sufficient. They sleep through the night. They can make their own beds. They can entertain themselves without causing much property damage. And Amy, the old Amy, the table-top-dancing, globetrotting, drinking-game-playing Amy is beginning to resurface. Sure, she doesn't exactly close down bars or bungee-jump off of bridges in foreign countries anymore, but she does stay up past ten now. And

the Octopus

she's been known to put away half a bottle of wine from time to time. And she kicks ass in Guitar Hero. She is a beacon of hope for new moms everywhere: We will not always be octopuses. We won't always be a bunch of Cybils, about to swoop in on our husbands when we see them cutting sandwiches the wrong way. Someday we will shed our layers of momminess and reemerge like butterflies, beautiful and full of promise, ready to reclaim our rightful personalities and stay up late.

But for now, we're pretty much screwed.

Chapter 14
The Switch

And speaking of screwed, I feel like we're close enough that I can now let you in on a little secret: Sometimes I wish I were a man.

Not in the sense that I would have to mow the yard, or shave my face or anything like that. But in a way, I am jealous of my husband. I wish my brain were wired more like his. I wish I had The Switch.

I'm talking about The Sexual Switch. The ability to turn desire on and off like a garden hose. One minute you're watching TV, minding your own business, then you see a flash of flesh on a Victoria Secret commercial and suddenly you're ready to go. Your Fun Zone lights up like a pinball machine, ready to knock around a few marbles. Screw making dinner, screw the kids sleeping in the next room, screw the blinds cracked just enough for a nosy neighbor to catch a show if he feels like peeping. You're randy and you're ready.

The closest I've come to having The Switch was way back in high school. Make-out parties. Getting geared up for a little first base, second base and so forth, only to have lights thrown on, coupled with the heavy, purposeful footsteps of an approaching parent down rickety basement stairs. If that doesn't wilt your lily, nothing will. But as soon as all was assumed well and kosher, as soon as the creak of the closing door reached your adolescent eardrums, the lights dimmed, music resumed, and the baseball game continued without missing a play.

I think having kids has ruined any chance I ever had of recapturing The Switch.

Like the other day when I decided my husband and I should take a bath. The kids were finally asleep, the wine was red and the night was young. A picture began taking shape in my head of the two of us luxuriating beneath the warm, fuzzy blanket of a million tiny bubbles, feeling my husband's body resting against mine, sipping our wine as we talked. I turned the faucet on hot, and dumped a whole bottle of bubble bath into the burbling water. I even turned on our old lava lamp, because after two kids, the glow from a blue, Spencer's novelty lamp is much more forgiving than the glare of eight naked bulbs screaming from the vanity.

My husband appeared, his Iphone set to a playlist of soft, sensuous songs, filling our bathroom with velvety music. We sank into the tub together, clinked glasses and let the hot water dissolve a week's worth of tension. I started to feel like a person again. A woman. And, dare I say, a bit frisky. That is, until the crackling monitor in the other room belted out the latest hit from our five-month-old daughter.

"Want me to get her?" my husband asked.

I sank lower in the tub and shook my head, determined not to let a few warbling cries upset my still-tentative libido. I focused on the music, the wine, my husband's scruffy face cast in a blue shadow, trying like hell to block out my daughter's whimpers. Already I felt the painfully narrow window of opportunity start to slip shut, as my modest sexual fantasies were replaced by my fantasy of climbing into bed and falling asleep to an episode of *No Reservations*.

The cries escalated to somewhere between whining and wailing.

My husband, who had fished my foot out from beneath the bubbles and begun massaging it, looked at me.

"You sure you don't want me to get her?"

I was sure. Because I knew that, though he would try his darnedest to get our daughter to settle back down (he wanted to get busy as much as I did…no wait, *a lot more* than I did), he would fail. I knew this because she was teething, and the only thing that *would* get her to settle down was to nurse. The reason I hadn't already leapt from the tub and beat a dripping, bubbly path to her door was that I knew once I'd transitioned to Mommy Mode, there was no going back.

The music stopped for a moment, and in that gap of silence came a huge, shuddering yowl of a baby who wasn't taking 'no' for an answer.

"All right, all right," I muttered, and pulled myself from the tub.

"I'll just hang out here," my husband called after me.

I sat in the rocking chair for just under twenty minutes, rocking and nursing my darling daughter back to sleep. More than enough time for my visions of intimacy to swirl down the drain with my now lukewarm bathwater. By the time I made it to my bedroom, my husband had relocated our wine to our respective night stands, brought in the lava lamp, and lay on the bed in just his boxers, smiling as if welcoming me to a really hot party.

I almost burst into tears right there; the last thing I wanted now was to hop into bed and play a little naked rodeo. And my husband looked so sweet, so openly eager to get down to business. How was I supposed to tell him that I was ready to crash? That our daughter had sucked my mojo out through my nipples, leaving me with the overwhelming urge to put on my most unflattering, wrinkled pajamas and call it a night? This was supposed to happen, dammit. The lava lamp was still on, for crying out loud.

My husband is a very understanding, rational person, but sometimes even he finds it cruelly unfair that my maternal self and my sexual self cannot occupy the same body at the same time. And when my maternal self comes to roost, her fat ass doesn't leave for days. Sometimes weeks.

I've spoken to friends, relatives, strangers in the mall, and all of them seem to agree about one thing: Children are thieving little monsters that rob us of our sex drives. Having a baby in the house is about as sexy as sharing a bed with a giant tortoise. The only light at the end of the, um, *tunnel* is knowing that this drought won't last. Someday our bodies will be more than a couple of feedbags attached to a jungle gym. Someday our husbands and we will get an hour or two of private time without being interrupted by a baby's wails or a toddler's nightmare.

So as long as our husband understands that we don't mind giving without receiving, we'll get through this dry spell and emerge on the other side ready to be reciprocated. And maybe by then we'll have something resembling a switch of our own.

Chapter 15
The Incredible Journey—To The Grocery Store

Okay, so let's talk about something that has absolutely nothing to do with sex for a second.

Wait! Come back! I promise, we'll get back to sex eventually. It's what got us into this in the first place, right? And since we're all starved for sex the way it used to be, we will take a little dirty talk wherever we can get it.

Instead, let's talk about the grocery store.

A normal person can make it to the grocery store for a gallon of milk in ten minutes. Parents are not normal. Parents of young children are especially not normal.

Even if in your previous life you were the most normal, vanilla, ordinary human being on the planet, if you have even one child, you are now in the abnormal club. Welcome.

If you want to go to the store around 10:00 in the morning, and you're planning to bring along your darling offspring, you need to start preparing early. A month in advance is ideal. First, you need to pack the diaper bag, and depending on the number of kids coming with you, that diaper bag might get a little heavy. Figure out the number of diapers you might need for your 45-minute outing and multiply that by four. Also, unless you want to hear children who swore up and down they weren't hungry when you left the house but the instant you pass the cookie aisle whine that they are starving to death, be sure to bring along a snack. Of course, you'll be in a grocery store. Don't be above pulling a bag of goldfish off the shelf and tearing it open to feed your ravenous little vultures as you shop (Note: Don't try doing this with M&Ms.).

If you have more than one pint-sized companion on your journey, multiply the amount of time you think you're going to spend at the store by eight hundred, especially if at least one of those offspring is not yet self-mobile. You'd think this would speed things up—you wouldn't have to chase after two or more children as they dash off toward the Lucky Charms or grab handfuls of those sample candies, completely ignorant to the coin box posted above them. However, it will be mighty difficult to corral even a relatively compliant little shopper when you have a sixteen-pound person strapped to your chest. Don't get me wrong—I love the Baby Bjorn, Baby Sling, or any other contraption that gives you hands-free parenting, but ever try to run while wearing one of those things? It's more awkward than a 7th grade dance, and twice as painful (unless you count the time Michael Haren abandoned me on the dance floor before *Patience* was all the way over...*that* was pretty painful...).

Also, don't forget toys. Especially if you have a boy. My son prefers Matchbox motorcycles, but even four-wheeled cars, airplanes, fingerboards, action figures; anything of that ilk will suffice. Because if a child has something wheeled in his little hands, the possibilities are endless. The store isn't a store anymore—it's a giant, endless track for his toy to ride on, fly over, run along, drive across, etc. Keep in mind, however, that depending on your child's strength and dexterity, you may spend much of your time replacing items his car knocks to the floor (replacing those skinny little boxes of Rice-a-Roni is especially time-consuming—those things are like dominoes waiting for the tiniest push to send them tumbling backwards).

So, you're ready to bundle everyone into the car. You've got your diaper bag with eighty diapers, enough food and drink to last you through the winter, a Christmas morning's worth of toys, you've got pacifiers, the little cover for your shopping cart seat (in case your children tire during the arduous trek up and down thirteen aisles) your Baby Bjorn, and of course, your reusable shopping bags. Just know that you will need a shopping cart before you even enter the store just to haul all of your gear. You'll almost have more stuff going *into* the store than coming out.

You drive the seven minutes it takes to get you to the store (after listening to a CD you used to like until your toddler insisted on listening to the same Radiohead song for the three-thousandth time and now you're ready to impale yourself on your shifter before the first track even starts), you pull into the parking lot, hop out of the car, strap your littlest into the Baby Bjorn, wrestle your other one or two into their shoes (which do not have to match or even be the right size—kids won't care, parents will care even less, and screw anyone else who feels like judging), and feel around the floor of your car for the diaper bag, cart cover and your purse. Where's your purse? Oh, crap.

Trip to the grocery store, Take Two…

Let's talk for a minute about shopping carts. They come in all different shapes, sizes, colors, makes, models, some have hydraulics, some come equipped with cup holders, some you can sit in right next to your kid and peddle yourself around the store like Fred Flintstone. Before I had Elsa, Rollie always sat in the front of the cart while I shopped. But the first time I brought both children to the store, I wasn't sure how to handle transporting them both around with

eating off the shelf at the store

yes   no

me. Being a newbie at the two-kid thing, I selected this monstrosity of a cart that looked normal except for this wide, yellow bench affixed to the front. I mean this was like a park bench. It would have comfortably accommodated three average-sized adults. My son clamored aboard and I strapped him in, then secured my daughter's carseat into the front of the cart, which was about ten feet away from where I was supposed to push. And we were off.

I felt like I was driving a semi through the store. People leaped out of my path as we approached. I practically had to signal when making a turn. The cart should have had one of those Caution: Wide Right Turns signs on it. After ramming into a display of soup cans and successfully destroying one of those little boxes that spits out coupons, I ditched the enormous cart somewhere in the meat department and fled with my kids back to the front, for a normal, nice, compact car of a cart. Elsa's carseat sat in the basket and Rollie sat in the front. Sure, I only had enough room left for one container of yogurt, but at least this cart didn't beep when I backed it up.

And so now you've selected the appropriate cart, and you've cleaned it with disinfectant wipes like a criminal getting rid of fingerprints. You've covered the seat, stashed your purse, your luggage, located the emergency exits and boarded your children. And you're ready to start shopping. Yay!

Grocery stores are arranged with parents in mind. I know many people out there would beg to differ, pointing out that the milk is all the way in the most inconvenient corner of the store, and that you practically have to dodge booby traps, poisoned darts and spear-wielding pygmies to reach it. But look at what you walk by to eventually get there.

First is the Bakery. The case of ornamental pastries, rolls and loaves of crusty bread that frame the holy grail for kids: Free Cookies.

Do not pass up the Free Cookies. Do not collect two hundred dollars. Do not torture yourself any more than you have to. I don't care if it's right before dinner, if your kid hasn't had anything to eat but Tootsie Rolls and fruit punch, if he has a mouth full of cavities and your dentist specifically warned you against sweets in general but Free Cookies from your grocery store's bakery in particular. Get your kid a Free Cookie. And while he's munching on it, get as much shopping done as you possibly can. Pretend you're on one of those game shows—*Supermarket Sweep*—and you have to load up your cart with as many necessities as you can before time runs out and the last bite of Free Cookie has been consumed. Pretend you are being chased by a hungry bear through the store, or a pack of wolves, or Steelers fans. Just hurry for God's sake. *Hurry*.

If, however, your child manages to shove the entire Free Cookie into his cute little pie-hole in five seconds or, like my son, takes one bite and drops it, make sure the next stop on your whirlwind tour is the deli. Even if you have plenty of lunchmeat, cheese, hard-boiled eggs and banana pudding in your house, make sure you stop at the deli. Get something. And then get a sample of that something for your kid. Even the smallest request, say, one-tenth of an ounce of salami, will warrant a free sample. And even if your kid hates salami and anything to do with it, if you dangle a little slice of meaty goodness in front of his nose, he won't be able to refuse.

I used to see moms pushing their children around in shopping carts, the children chattering at mach one, firing all sorts of requests and questions out, and the mom just staring blankly at the shelf and uttering an 'uh-huh,' every now and then. I remember thinking how awful it was that the mother wasn't paying any attention to her child, how sad it was that she was missing out on interacting with her offspring because she was trying to figure out where the hell the Crisco was. I remember thinking, *when I have a kid, I won't ignore him like that*. So hilarious to look back on my smug, twenty-something internal monologue. Like I knew anything about anything.

It's deceiving, really, watching a mother shop with her kids. She may look like she's catatonic, but really her brain is burning enough fuel to single-handedly melt a few polar ice caps. She's using both sides of it, really. The side responsible for reading labels, performing math equations and deducing the pros and cons of any given purchase, and the side responsible for keeping her toddler from tearing open a box of dog biscuits and helping himself to some. It's a wonder any mother leaves the grocery store with her sanity, much less the three things she went in there for (and the thirty-five things she's leaving with, including Pop-Tarts, cookie dough, a Matchbox car and a box of wine). I saw a special once where people shopping for groceries had electrodes attached to their heads and scientists monitored their brainwaves to see what sort of synapses take place when said shopper encountered certain items. It was really something. The brainwave activity was likened to a person solving higher math equations, dissecting literature, conducting complicated experiments, performing piano concertos. And that's just when there aren't any sales going on. Imagine what goes on in a person's mind when, say, Steamfresh veggies are Buy One, Get One or cans of tuna are 2 for $3.00. That's when you have to start using your third grade math. Let's see, how many times does 2 go into 3? How many ounces are in a pound? How many low-fat cookies can I eat before I can't zip up my jeans?

And now let's look at the brain waves of someone shopping during a sale with 2 kids in tow. The printout would look like a magnitude 9.9 earthquake. Or, depending on how long the person spent in the store and what stage of consciousness the children were in (see Chapter 18, Levels Of Consciousness Not Achieved With Chemical Substances) the brainwave activity might be completely flat, indicating the person has mentally checked out.

Oftentimes after a productive round of grocery shopping, I feel hung over—drained, tired and slightly nauseated. Not only am I reading labels, shelf tags, trying desperately to remember if we need creamed corn, or if that was the one item I stocked up on recently and now have ten cans of it in our pantry. I will literally agonize over such decisions, all the while trying to maintain a conversation with my son, who likes to point out pretty much everything he sees and knows the word for, and entertaining my daughter, who has grown bored with watching her own hand open and close like she's on an acid trip and is starting to fuss.

It's exhausting keeping all of these things going at once. But it does explain how I do end up with all that creamed corn and no bread. One lapse in focus and suddenly I forget my own name and decide that I really do need one more can.

Another thing I've noticed since having kids is that I now purchase obscene amounts of food, and have hardly made a dent in my supply when I suddenly have the urge to go get more. My pantry is always full-to-overflowing, sometimes with stuff I don't think I'll ever even use, like fruit cocktail, tapioca, and commemorative boxes of Florida State frosted flakes. I am at the grocery store so often the cashiers and I have the same menstrual cycle, and my son has started calling the storeowner Uncle Publix.

I guess my need to stock up on food can be traced back to the whole 'gatherer' instinct. But this really didn't kick in until after I had kids. When it was just my husband and me, I really didn't find it necessary to have five packages of goldfish on our shelves, or a months' supply of cereal bars. But I find it comforting to open our pantry and know that if we are ever trapped in the house because say, a flock of vultures descends upon our roof (which actually happens in my neighborhood…I guess because of all the retirees) and we can't leave out of fear of being either pecked to death or pooped upon, we wouldn't starve. We could subsist for an entire spring on creamed corn alone.

Chapter 16
I Spy A Bar—Be Right Back, Kids

I have determined that the rules we set with our children are only in place so that they can be completely disregarded when we take our children on long trips.

Specifically car trips, but any type of travel would apply here—air travel (which we'll get to), trains, ships, horse-drawn carriage. Any time during which your child must sit in one spot for more than twenty minutes at a stretch counts as a long trip.

Take TV, for example. Normally my child does not watch *Wall-E* three times in a row while drinking a can of soda and wearing only a diaper and a t-shirt. But if we're going to be in a car for seven hours, sure. Have another lollipop. Another French fry. Anything to keep you from kicking the back of my seat or engaging in that specific pitch of whine that I swear to God was genetically engineered to strike a vomit-inducing chord in only *my* eardrum.

This phenomenon of controlled anarchy when traveling for an

extended period also applies to the companions of the traveling child. One summer a few years ago, my sister and I drove from Atlanta to North Carolina with our respective children—hers were six, four and ten months and my son was five months. Her boys wanted to stop at South of the Border, that infamous and fabulously tacky truck stop on the border of North and South Carolina. Going against every fiber of our beings, we obliged because, as you know by now, we were on a long journey and no longer possessed the ability to reason with or deny our children anything. They could have been asking to stop at a nudie bar that served a buffet of cotton candy and we would have shrugged and said, *why the hell not?*

And so there we were, my sister and me, sitting on the curb of one of the souvenir shops at South of the Border, wearing cut-off shorts, drinking Yoo-hoo that was quickly growing warm, and nursing our infants while we watched her sons sword-fight with a pair of matching South of the Border back-scratchers. Yes siree. We were the quintessential model of two mothers who had temporarily lost their minds. Maybe it was the July heat, the Yoo-hoo, the stir-craziness of being trapped in a cramped car for seven hours and listening to the boys' *Lion King* video for the fifth time. Whatever it was, it made us decide that breast-feeding in a South of the Border truck stop parking lot was a perfectly sane thing to do.

We do everything to keep our children happy during car rides. If that means we have to contort our body to reach fallen books, toys, crayons, pacifiers, grapes, sippy cups, while keeping our hand on the wheel going ninety-five on the freeway because we want to reach our destination before the next meltdown or exploded diaper, then by God, so be it. We will sacrifice our own needs, cross our legs and watch rest areas and exits whiz past because our angel is sleeping and we can't possibly consider stopping the car to wake them just because we drank five gallons of Diet Coke to stay awake so we wouldn't have to drive during normal waking hours and now it feels like an elephant is sitting on our bladder. We will listen to the same stupid Disney movie, sing the same songs, play I Spy until our creative wells are exhausted. We will buy our children milkshakes and ice cream and bags of candy just to keep their mouths busy and happy. We will come up with a hundred different answers to Are We There Yet, try a hundred different distractions, and even try to keep our language in check when a-holes tail us too closely so that our children don't remember the car ride when Mommy dropped a bunch of f-bombs.

Our children have it made. They have no idea how long car trips used to be. How I remember, stuffed in the third row of my father's 1975 Plymouth Malibu station wagon with my sister, various bags and suitcases encroaching on what precious little space I had on my side of the seat, my legs sticking to the vinyl as the AC struggled to make it back to us, forgotten and ignored, and left to duke out our battles over seat space on our own. How I sat, sweaty and cramped, suffering the blows of punch-buggy reds, catching only snippets of conversations going on in the happy, cool, front section of the car. Back in the days when Walkmen were luxuries, when the only form of entertainment for us was Name That Roadkill or placing bets on how far we would get before a.) Someone's belongings were blown off the roof rack or b.) The car broke down.

Without a doubt, our children will never know the true beauty of the family road trip.

Air travel is a different story. Having never flown with my family as a kid, I don't have any miserable experiences from childhood to reflect upon. I will say that any of you who choose to fly with your children, especially if your children are still in diapers, are, in fact, totally nuts.

I'm allowed to say this—in a brief moment of insanity, *I* decided to fly to Atlanta alone with Rollie and Elsa. *How bad could it be?* I reasoned. I'd flown alone with Rollie from Florida to Portland…six hours…pregnant…without buying him his own ticket. And while that is something I'd rather not do again, I—in all my smug, naiveté—figured that taking a 45-minute flight with two kids would be a piece of cake.

First we had to check in. I was only checking one bag, to simplify the security screening more than anything. The idea of wrangling two children out of shoes and stuffing diaper bags and carseats through the conveyor belt on top of assuring the TSA worker that the ominous-looking tub of Noxzema was not explosive in nature simply did not appeal to me. It was worth the 20 bucks to send my saline solution and shampoo on to Atlanta without me.

Attempting to coax Rollie through the metal detector, however, was a bit of a challenge. I guess I should be glad that he doesn't instantly warm up to strangers. Or do what they ask. Or do what *I* ask while they stand smiling on the other side of a scary-looking, door-shaped rectangle that beeps and lights up like a giant, terrifying baby toy.

The security people were pretty understanding though. They made me feel somewhat less inept than usual as I struggled to remove my own belt and shoes, manhandled Elsa from her stroller and pleaded with Rollie to hurry up and take off his shoes because the line was starting to build up behind us like dorky ticket-holders for the opening night re-release of *Star Wars*. They held out hands for Rollie to high-five, they cooed at Elsa, they tested the carseat for bomb-making residue with the utmost courtesy. Only twenty dirty looks from other passengers later, we were through the screening and on our merry way to Gate A1.

Rollie was pretty excited about riding on an airplane. He pointed out each one he saw, asking if *that* was the one we would be taking, asking why it *wasn't* the one we would be taking, asking where was the one we *would* be taking, and wanting to know when we could get on the one we would be taking. It was great fun answering every version of every question he could think up while trying to navigate my loaded-down sit-and-stand through the airport, trying to

keep the carseat that balanced precariously atop our eighty pieces of carry-on from toppling onto Elsa, who was in the front seat, angrily kicking her feet, getting frustrated that her socks wouldn't come off.

Needless to say, as soon as we boarded, I was ready to administer the Benadryl and order myself a ten-dollar mini-bottle of wine.

At least the airline employees came through once again. I'd been fretting all morning about the logistics of loading Rollie, Elsa, our bags and the carseat onto a quickly filling airplane, but as soon as I made it down the jet-way, a flight attendant appeared and happily hauled the twenty-pound toddler seat down the aisle, cheerily barging into other passengers as she pushed forward to our seat. I followed her like I was following a linebacker through a throng of football players, Elsa clutched to me like a precious pigskin.

Once I had my children settled, a woman appeared in the aisle, studying her ticket.

"I think I'm right here," she said, dropping her purse into the seat beside me.

Poor thing, I thought. This was going to be the longest 45 minutes of her life.

You can always tell who on an airplane has children. They're the ones who don't shoot death-rays at the parents of screaming toddlers. They ask nicely to have you keep your kid from kicking their seat. They don't look suicidal when they realize they're stuck in the same row as you and your colicky infant. They offer to help. They offer to change seats. They offer carry your bags. They've been there. They know how bad it sucks.

Take the woman beside me. I was trying to set up Rollie's DVD player (which I highly recommend), and she offered to hold Elsa for me. Then she started playing Peek-a-boo with her. She had Elsa chuckling for a full ten minutes, even after I had loaded *Cars* for Rollie and he was already staring slack-jawed at the screen. When I opened up a sippy cup at thirty thousand feet and apple juice went spraying all over her, the woman only smiled and said, "That's happened to me before!" She was practically ready to breastfeed Elsa for me. It was great.

And at the end of the flight, after I waited for everyone to deplane, some strapping young lad offered to carry the carseat back up the aisle for me. I felt special, half-celebrity, half-paraplegic, someone everyone feels sorry for and wants to help and commiserates with and smiles at. I can't imagine traveling with two kids, being pregnant and having some other super-power, like really big knockers. People would be falling all over themselves to help me tie my shoes. They would offer the shirt off their back, their bottom dollar, their left arm, just to open a door for me. Sure it would be out of pity (and because my boobs would be bigger then most items in the produce department). I'd still take it.

Chapter 17
Liar Liar, Diaper On Fire

I don't know when it happens, but sometime between birth and a kid's transition into speech, he figures out how to lie.

Mainly these lies will be innocuous. They will mostly center on whether or not your child is walking around in a dirty diaper. You can ask your child if he is poopy, and despite all evidence to the contrary (the scent, the ass of said diaper drooping to his knees, the fact that you noticed him standing very still behind the couch for about five minutes) he will tell you that he's not.

I haven't figured this one out yet. Why do kids automatically say no to this question? It can't be pleasant, going about your daily rituals in your own filth, having a cloud of methane following you around, being unable to actually sit down and get anything done. They must understand that you are the one who's going to remedy the problem, that all they have to do is confirm that they are indeed poopy, and you will swoop right in with the wipes and the clean diaper and take care of things for them. Yet *no* is their answer of choice.

Could it be fear that motivates them to lie? Do they think that answering yes will send you into a Joan Crawford-esque tirade, that you will scream at them and belittle them and refuse to change their diaper—they'll just have to suffer the consequences of being unable to use the toilet? Or maybe shame is the driving force. Maybe they are embarrassed that they are poopy, because they know full well where to go when they have to take care of business, but just can't be bothered with such things when nature calls.

Whatever the reason, soon the question of whether they are poopy isn't the only thing they are lying about. Soon they'll lie about breaking your favorite mug, or coloring on your coffee table, or cutting their own bangs (I myself am guilty of this particular crime—when asked who cut my bangs brutally short and uneven, I claimed that I had no idea who did it—some masked man armed with a pair of pinking shears had barged into my room, snipped my hair, and disappeared into the night).

Lucky for me, Rollie hasn't started lying about anything but the status of his diaper (oh yeah, and whether or not he has to go to the bathroom). And I'm trying to avoid having him feel like he has to lie for as long as possible.

Like today, I was in the kids' bathroom and noticed that the entire box of tissues we keep on top of the toilet tank was soggy. Upon closer inspection I also noticed several sopping wet tissues on the floor around the toilet, and water droplets on the toilet seat. At first I thought my husband had gotten the box wet when he took a shower (we're in the process of re-grouting our shower...have been for three weeks now...another thing about having kids—household projects either take ten times as long to complete, or simply don't get done at all). But then Rollie wandered by the open door, and suddenly I had an awful premonition.

"Rollie," I called.

His adorable little blond head appeared in the doorway. "Yes, Mama?"

I picked up the box and held it out for him to see. "What happened to these tissues?"

He looked from me to the box and back, clearly trying to gauge my demeanor.

"They're all wet," he said.

"Yes, I see that. Why are they all wet?"

And I'm assuming that since I didn't seem to be angry with him, he pointed at the toilet. "They were in the potty."

"Oh," I said, instantly grossed out that I was handling the box. "Did *you* put them in the potty?"

"Yep," he wandered closer and peered at them. "They're all wet, Mama."

"You put them in the potty and then took them out?"

"Yep."

I was very aware of how careful I needed my next words to be. Do I scold him for doing something both totally disgusting and potentially messy (thank God he hadn't tried to flush the box down the toilet)? What if he decides to start lying to avoid making me mad? Soon he'll be putting other, less obvious things in the toilet and pulling them out…Elsa's pacifier…car keys… my contact lens case. And he'll learn to be stealthy and avoid detection. And then the next time I put in my contacts, I'll wonder why they sting and smell like Scrubbing Bubbles. And when I ask him if he put Mommy's contact lenses in the potty, he'll merely look up at me with those innocent gray eyes and say, *No Mommy. I didn't.*

"Let's not put anything but toilet paper in the potty from now on," I said. And even then, it somehow seemed wrong. If Rollie ends up being a

couch-diving, money-borrowing pot-head, I'll trace it back to the time when I discovered a wet box of Puffs Plus and was too freaking *nice* about it, just so I could squeeze a few months' worth of honesty out of the kid.

Or maybe lying is inevitable. Maybe it's just part of every child's learning process. Maybe they don't lie just to get away with stuff, but for lots of other reasons. I know when I was a kid, I used to lie for attention. I made up all sorts of stories about how I had to go the hospital to have a splinter removed, or that I was late for school because I had to help my parents catch a rat in our attic. Occasionally I'd lie to keep from getting caught (and from getting a dreaded Spanking—see Chapter 6, Why 'Because I Said So' Is A Perfectly Acceptable Reason) but for the most part, my lies were a vehicle of entertainment for the listener, and an attempt to get some recognition in a world that, in my eight-year-old mind, failed to notice how awesome I was.

And now that I *have* kids, I'm sorry to admit that I am still a big, fat, liar.

I think this is part of being a mom—for the longest time I truly believed that my parents were going to buy me a horse. And not just buy me a horse, but also build a fence in our backyard to keep the horse contained. For years I envisioned a beautiful brown horse with a white nose sleeping in my playhouse, and in the morning coming to my window, where I would lean out and feed it carrots for breakfast and stroke his long muzzle, and then leap from my windowsill and onto his broad back so he could take me to school. I imagined how jealous my classmates would be as they climbed off of the boring yellow school bus, and here I'd come galloping up astride my very own horse.

It was my mother who fanned the flames of this fantasy. I distinctly remember having several discussions with her about the possibility of our getting a horse.

Me: Mom, can we get a horse?

My Mom: We'll see.

Me (*the wheels already spinning*): Could we keep him in the backyard?

My Mom: Maybe. It's big enough for one.

Me: Would we need a barn?

My Mom: Your playhouse is big enough for a horse.

Me: When can we get one?

My Mom: I don't know. I've always wanted a horse.

Me (*hardly believing my luck that here, all this time, my mother and I both wanted a horse and now here we were, having an actual discussion about the possibility of getting one. To an eight-year-old girl, that's as good as a yes*): Me, too.

Needless to say, I'm still waiting for my mom to make good on that little promise.

But the other day, I found myself having a similar discussion with Rollie. He wasn't asking for anything as elaborate as a hoofed animal for a pet, but the intensity of his desire for a Lightning McQueen remote control car was very familiar. As was my response...

Rollie (*as we walk down the toy aisle at Target*): Lightning McQueen!

Me: I see him.

Rollie: Can I have him please, Momma?

Me: You don't really need him, baby.

Rollie: He goes super fast!

Me: Yes he does.

Rollie (*now removing the Lightning McQueen car from the shelf and walking toward our cart with it*): Can I have him, Momma?

Me: Not today, Rollie. Maybe another time.

Cut!

I know damn well I'm never going to buy this remote control car for my son because a.) He has a bajillion cars at home, b.) This Lightning McQueen fetish is a phase he is currently at the pinnacle of, and so if I were to wait until say, Christmas to buy this thing, he will play with it for a total of five seconds before either he gets sick of it or it breaks, and c.) If I said yes to every impulse-buy of his, I'd already be in some serious credit card debt.

But the phrase *Not Today*...therein lies the problem. Not Today leaves open the possibility of tomorrow, and every other subsequent day from now until he gets a job and can buy his own toys. Not Today leaves a sliver of hope. Not Today's main function is to cut off any tantrum, bout of begging or other such spectacle before it even begins. But Not Today, to a two-year-old, is also as good as a *Yes*.

Yet I find myself using Not Today or a variation thereof in all kinds of situations. If he asks for a trip to the beach and I have no intention of taking him, I say "Maybe." If he wants to watch *Cars* (again), but if I have to hear Lightning McQueen say "Ka-CHOW" one more time I'm going to stab myself in the ear with a Crazy Straw, I say "Not right now." Which of course, to a two-year-old, means "Any time after Now." Which is why he asks again two minutes later. Sigh.

And that's not all I lie about. I tell him the orange scribbles on his paper look exactly like the dinosaur he said he drew. I tell him he did a great job putting his pants on even though they're on backwards and both of his legs are shoved into one pant-leg. I let him believe in Santa Claus, the Easter Bunny, that birdies and lizards that cross his path are saying hello to him. It's no wonder kids his age are completely egocentric. It's parents like me who perpetuate that attitude.

But in all fairness, I understand why we do it. Why we lie. I understand that we do it to keep our children happy, to protect them from the ugly truths in life. Kids have plenty of time to figure it out without us telling them they suck at getting dressed or can't draw for crap.

I, however, am still waiting for my pet horse....

Chapter 18
Levels Of Consciousness Not Achieved With Chemical Substances

Every evening in households across the country, parents experience the Golden Moment. The moment when the sea of brightly colored plastic is piled in the toy box, the bath toys are dripping in the corner of the tub, the air smells of baby lotion and bubblegum toothpaste, the last page has been read, the last song has been sung, the night lights come on and children are sleeping peacefully in the soft glow of their rotating planetarium, dreaming of the day behind them and the one ahead.

You can almost hear a collective *Woo-Hoo!* echo through darkened neighborhoods as parents collapse onto couches, clink glasses together and celebrate a precious hour or two alone with their spouses. They settle in front of the TV or read books side by side on a comfy love seat, completely forgetting they have children as they soak in the glory of post-bedtime tranquility.

That is, until a blur passes by the doorway. A short, pajama-clad blur.

Is it me, or do kids think that we parents are scheming to steal their souls the second they close their eyes? I know Rollie guards his own consciousness like priceless treasure, greedily refusing to relinquish any waking moments, always wanting one more song, one more story, one more kiss, anything to extend his daytime world of wide-eyed awareness until he literally cannot keep his head from lolling and no longer has the energy to swallow instead of drool.

Throughout the day, children go through several stages leading up to unconsciousness. This transition takes place all day, sometimes slowly, sometimes all at once, and sometimes in an order so random it defies logic:

Awake and Normal. This is the one stage when a child is coherent, amiable, pleasant and can almost be mistaken for a human being. Usually lasting only forty-five minutes to an hour, this stage is obviously the most desirable, and therefore the most fleeting.

Borderline Functional. This stage can immediately follow Awake and Normal, although it may come and go without warning or reason. Borderline Functional may still display some of the Awake and Normal attributes (will accept food or drink, will brush teeth or put away toys), but requests to do these things will be met with more resistance (food or drink must be brightly colored and sugary and served in a highly specific manner—on a Wall-E plate or in a cup that lights up and plays music. This is not the time to introduce broccoli or anything somewhat healthy. Also, don't be surprised if you find yourself pleading with a Borderline Functional to clean up his toys. Like literally on your hands and knees because you are two seconds away from cleaning up the toys yourself, either to expedite the process, or to prevent the B.F. from morphing into the dreaded third stage):

Whining. This stage is when all normal functions start to break down, when the child's facial muscles can no longer produce even the tiniest grin no matter how goofy you act. The best way to identify a toddler in this third stage is tone of voice. When your child's voice makes you think he's been possessed by a mosquito, when any previous command he had of the English language is abandoned, as he seems to be speaking in tongues. *Use your words* is a phrase you will often find yourself repeating, though when your child has entered this stage, anything *you* say translates into a garbled, malevolent request that may or may not result in your child bursting into tears. This is when you know your child has arrived at the next stage:

Over-Tired. We can break this stage into two sub-stages. Your child's disposition will determine which sub-stage he falls into, although some children will vacillate between the two, or in special cases, occupy both at the same time.

Over-Tired Silly. This stage is when appendages flail for no apparent reason, when any instructions bounce off the child like pebbles off bulletproof glass. This is also the stage that will most likely result in a trip to the ER. Mainly because while there is normally little regard for his own well being, when a child is Over-Tired Silly, there is absolutely none. When he might normally use caution while scaling his baby gate, when he is Over-Tired Silly, all bets are off. Distance judgment becomes severely impaired or vanishes completely; while a child in the Awake and Normal phase might see a three-foot leap from the coffee table to the couch as risky and dangerous, an Over-Tired Silly child sees it as an absolute hoot, and will perform the jump over and over until he either injures himself and becomes Over-Tired Miserable (read on), or you scream *I can't take it anymore* and retreat to your bathtub with an entire bottle of wine.

The Over-Tired Silly child may also begin substituting every other word with one that is generally reserved for bathroom discussions. This is an actual conversation I had with my son during the Over-Tired Silly stage:

Me: Come on, Rollie, let's get your jammies on.

Rollie: No, let's get my *poopy* on.

Me (*sighing*): Rollie, that doesn't even make any sense, now come on.

Rollie: No jammies.

Me: You have to wear your jammies, it's night-night time.

Rollie (*giggling*): It's pee-pee time.

Me (*instantly thrilled at the prospect of my son announcing that he has to use the bathroom on his own instead of me having to badger him about it for hours and hours*): Do you have to use the potty first?

Rollie: My bottom.

Me: What about your bottom?

Rollie (*grinning*): Poopy on my bottom.

Me: You have poopy on your bottom? Seriously?

Rollie: Poop on the potty.

Me (*hearing the heavens open and a multitude of angels singing Handel's Hallelujah Chorus*): Okay, then. Let's get you on the potty! Yay!

Rollie: No, I want to eat it.

Me (*the angels abruptly silent*): You want to eat what?

Rollie (*laughing loudly now*): Poopy!

Me (*sighing again*): Rollie, that's really gross.

Rollie: I want to eat poopy.

Me: Trust me, you don't.

Rollie: I want to eat pee-pee.

Me: You don't eat pee-pee, you drink it.

Rollie: I want to *drink* pee-pee.

Me: Well, you can't have anything else to eat or drink, you already brushed your teeth. So come over here and put on your jammies right NOW.

Rollie (*now laughing hysterically*): Put my *poopy* on.

And while the Over-Tired Silly stage is annoying, exhausting yet somehow kind of amusing all at once, it is by far a better stage to deal with than…

Over-Tired Miserable. This stage is exactly as it sounds. Your child is over-tired and he is making you miserable. He's miserable, too, of course, but Over-Tired Miserable has a Midas effect. Everything and everyone an Over-Tired Miserable child touches will also become miserable. This is when tears spring forth if the child is so much as breathed on the wrong way. When any suggestion is met with a 'no,' even if you're suggesting a visit to Santa Claus himself coupled with a promise that every wish and dream the child has ever had is about to come true. This is the absolute last stop on the express train to Unconsciousness-ville. Not much can be done with an Over-Tired Miserable, except to deposit him in the nearest bed and hope sleep comes soon. And then you can have a drink, because anyone dealing with an Over-Tired Miserable child for any amount of time deserves to be richly rewarded. In my book, that means with alcohol. Big surprise.

Remember that these stages do not necessarily come in order, and that sometimes the order in which they come makes absolutely no sense. One minute you could be enjoying some nice, parent-child time with an Awake and Normal child, building a tower or coloring a picture, and suddenly, wham, you've got an Over-Tired Miserable on your hands, coming apart at the seams like a sweater from Wet Seal. But don't be discouraged. It's not you. It's the age. At least, that's what I tell myself, right after I bundle my weeping son into bed, put the baby gate across his door for the final time and crack open a beer.

Here endeth the second lesson. Amen.

Chapter 19
Guide To Half-Assed Cleaning

When I was growing up, my mother had a very peculiar style of cleaning the house. Occasionally after using the bathroom, I would notice an odd-looking powder sprinkled in the sink. Without giving it much thought, I would wash it down the drain, ignorant to the intention behind this ritual. What she was trying to do was leave a hint for someone to take the initiative to scrub the sinks with the Comet she'd deposited, but she was barking up the wrong tree with us. We simply thought she had intended to clean the sinks herself but was interrupted before she could finish. Silly us.

Or I would come home from school to find that the clothes I had left scattered on my floor were now piled in a corner chair with a towel thrown over them, as if the towel were hiding some mysterious sculpture I'd been laboring over for months. The sight of this lump on my chair never failed to enrage me, but it also left me baffled. Why on earth would my mother do this? Why not just leave the clothes on the floor, or better yet, put them in my laundry basket if the sight of them lying around bothered her so much? If she was worried

about offending visitors, how much better was it for a person to walk by and see a huge, amorphous lump in my chair than to see my room resemble an explosion in the junior department of JC Penney's?

My mother brought this draping technique into the kitchen, too. If the sink was piled with dirty dishes, my mother simply placed a dishrag over the contents of the sink, thus shielding any innocent passerby from the horrifying sight of the aftermath of an eight-person-family dinner. Instead of getting carpets cleaned, she bought smaller rugs to lay on top of unsightly stains or traffic marks. Wallpaper was painted over, and paint was wall-papered over, thus disguising handprints, paw prints, crayon scribbles and chair scrapes and everything else that happens to walls. I'm pretty sure we owned a vacuum cleaner, because I remember it disrupting my Saturday morning cartoons, sending static crackling across the TV screen whenever she happened to turn it on. But I never actually saw her use it.

Before I had kids, I thought perhaps my mom was just on the lazy side, never really making time to clean the house properly. Of course, now I know better.

Having kids means that you will now spend much of your time cleaning up after them. But note that 'cleaning up after' someone does not equate to actual *cleaning*. It's more like picking up after them, wiping up after them, doing everything you can to keep your house from looking like a landfill for the Island of Misfit Toys. Legos, Matchbox cars, balls of various sizes and shapes; it's like your children are leaving a trail of toys merely so they can find their way back to their rooms.

You may spend a lot of time *noticing* things that need to be cleaned, but not a lot of time actually *cleaning* anything. So when you actually get a moment to clean something properly, just worry about the basics. Vacuuming can make a house that might be declared a biohazard suddenly look as tidy as a putting green. And you can dust, but you may want to employ what I like to think of as the Indiana Jones Method: Blow. Just blow on the dust, watch it swirl around in the sunlight, and *then* vacuum. In the bathrooms, instead of using a sponge and some 409 to wipe down the counters, you may want to consider using a wad of dampened toilet paper. In a pinch of course. If your two-year-old has been coughing all over the place, please use the former means of cleaning. But if no one in your house is sick, and your mother-in-law is popping in for a visit, don't hesitate to reach for the TP. The aesthetic results will be identical.

Which brings us to laundry. Yes, it never ends. For a while, I was convinced that my clothes were having sex. It was the only explanation for what was happening in my laundry room. I honestly believed that somewhere in there a shirt, or perhaps a pair of undies, had a stash of Barry White albums, and as soon as I turned out the lights and shut the door, it fished out one of the albums, stuck it inside a hidden CD player, and to the deep, smooth croons of Mr. White, on top of the washer set to the spin cycle, my clothes had an orgy. (See? I told you we'd talk about sex again!)

And when I returned to swap the clothes into the dryer, I swear to you that my piles of clothes had multiplied. Socks I didn't remember even owning were popping up in strange places, shirts I swore I'd given away were returning like polyester boomerangs, waiting to be folded and placed inside a dresser drawer, where they would likely have more sex. One particular pair of my husband's shorts, ones I knew I'd thrown into the garbage at least twice because they were holier than a Baptist choir, reappeared in the dryer, acting all innocent, as if I'd never really intended to get rid of them—they'd fallen into the garbage can accidentally. I became kind of afraid of them…afraid that if I tried to toss them in the trash one more time they'd come back and smother me in my sleep.

The hamper is never empty, either. I don't think I've ever seen the bottom of it. Maybe there isn't one. Maybe where a bottom should be is really a portal into another dimension, where mountains of jeans, tank-tops and footie-pajamas are waiting for their window, their chance to leap into my laundry basket and get busy with whatever clothing is already there.

You will never do more laundry than you will once you have children. And not just because you have more clothes to wash. Before children I didn't have to change clothes two seconds after getting dressed because I'd just been spit-up on. I didn't have to wash piles of Kool-Aid stained t-shirts or bibs encrusted with bananas. And I never had to wash my own sheets because of spilled chocolate milk or boogies because God forbid my son actually use a tissue to wipe his nose. I should buy stock in Tide and Downy; I go through it by the barrel.

It's only gonna get worse. Soon Rollie will be at the age when boys think rolling around in the mud is the most fantastically fun thing they've ever done or will ever do in their lives. He'll start coming home with bloodstained pant-legs and marker on his sleeves. And Elsa, who knows what sort of havoc she'll wreak on her pretty little pink outfits. I'm seriously considering dressing my children completely in black for the next ten years. Sure they'll look like creepy little Goth kids, but at least they won't be sporting stubborn ketchup stains.

So remember, kids. Blow on dust, wipe with TP, and when in doubt, pile everything into a corner and drape a towel over it. And please, people, spay and neuter your laundry!

Chapter 20
Apple Dapple Purse

Since we're on the subject of cleaning, let's also tackle another sad, sad truth about being a mom:

Nothing you own will ever be nice again.

It doesn't matter if you're meticulous and anal and have always *always* kept things free of stains, dents, holes, or smears of peanut butter and jelly. Once you have kids, everything you own will soon look like you either a.) snatched it from the end of someone's driveway on garbage day or b.) got it from the Salvation Army. Your coffee table will soon be covered in little scratches from Thomas's wooden wheels, your TV will be coated in ubiquitous finger prints, and don't even bother looking at your carpet for the next fifteen years; it will only depress you.

Your clothing and accessories are no exception. Take purses, for example. My mother kept a disgusting purse. As a kid, I was always wary of digging through it, even if the situation was dire (i.e., I was scrounging for lunch

Apple Dapple Purse

money as the school bus barreled down the street). Mixed in with the oxidized pennies and expired coupons would be a few cough drops sans wrappers, bobby pins, crumpled tissues, melted gum, inkless pens, loose buttons, and a half-roll of peppermint Lifesavers (never a whole roll—for much of my childhood I believed that half-rolls were the only way Lifesavers came). And after counting out as much change as I could scrape up, I'd dash to the bus stop, picking black gunk out from under my fingernails as I ran.

I always swore I would never let my purse get as nasty as my mother's. And for years I kept that promise. I made it through my twenties with a purse that was uncluttered, more or less. Maybe the occasional gum wrapper or paper clip would make its way into the depths, but it never stayed long. I prided myself on my clean purse—you wouldn't have to paw through a bunch of miscellaneous crap to find a few nickels in *my* handbag. No sir-ee.

And then I had kids.

I dug through my purse for my keys the other day, and came up with a handful of Apple Jacks. Not even whole, fresh Apple Jacks (which, I assure you, would have been bad enough). No, these were smashed, stale, *generic* Apple Jacks. Apple Dapples, I think they're called.

"What the…." I looked into my purse, half-expecting to find a cockroach or two gorging themselves on whatever other vittles were within. I fished out a little pink sock, a lint-covered pacifier, a dried-out baby wipe, and a Matchbox car (I swear those things multiply. If you buy even one for your son or daughter, you'll end up with an entire fleet, every make, model and color of every car ever dreamed up). I had to face the horrible truth: After years of vigilance, of dutifully cleaning out my bag almost daily, I had finally succumbed to the Mom Purse Affliction. I don't know how or when it happened, but there it was, a disgustingly messy purse, complete with the mysterious black gunk that lodged itself under my fingernails.

I cannot tell you how thankful I was that my husband was not around to witness this—despite my insistence that I have a relatively tidy purse, he refuses to go in there for anything, insisting just as strongly that it is a portable landfill. And now he'd be right. My purse will never be the same.

This is also true about my car. Before children, my car was beautiful, immaculate, and pristine. Once in a while an offending bug would grace the windshield, a bird would unceremoniously poop on the roof, a few CD cases would be stashed in the center console. It even retained its New Car Smell, despite being several years old.

Now, however…good God. The outside is never clean—washing it myself is a bigger production than a Broadway rendition of *High School Musical*. I have to break out the portacrib and toys for Elsa, drag out the wading pool for Rollie, make sure every item either one could possibly need in the next hour is in the garage so I don't have to run inside for it—diapers, wipes, drinks, snacks, burp cloths, pacifiers, towels. It turns into an all-morning affair, and that's if everyone is in a good mood. There have been many times that I've been tempted, in a heavy downpour, to simply douse my car in Palmolive and let Mother Nature make herself useful.

The inside of my car is another story. A sad, painful story. If you set a raccoon loose in my car, it would be sustained for days. Unless it found the stash of edibles stuffed inside the center buckle of my son's car seat. Then it would be *weeks* before the little critter had an empty stomach. Just a word of advice regarding snacks in the car: always get vanilla flavored anything instead of chocolate. And always have baby wipes everywhere you can possibly keep them. I've been amazed at what those things will clean—juice, chocolate, lollipop residue, wine, every conceivable bodily fluid. That's what the commercials should emphasize—cleaning a little baby bottom is probably number seven on the top ten uses for wipes.

God forbid I ever get, say, robbed at a stop sign or some such scenario. I can just imagine the robber standing outside the driver's side window demanding money.

"Hold on," I'll say, as I dig through the wasteland of books, shoes, toys, and assorted baby accoutrement for my purse, only to have to paw through goldfish, tissues, pacifiers and crayons for my wallet. And only *then* to find that I have no cash at all, and I left my credit card in my son's pocket, having stuck it there after letting him swipe it through the machine at the grocery store because that was the only way to keep him from destroying the Tic Tac display in the checkout line. And my son will inevitably be sleeping, since being strapped in his car seat is the only time he sits still long enough to take a nap. And I'll turn back to the robber and ask if he'll settle for a handful of smashed Apple Dapples. Although by then he will have already given up and decided to mess with someone who doesn't have kids. They're easy to spot. They're the ones with tidy purses and clean cars.

Chapter 21
The Quick And...The Not-So-Quick

As you've probably already figured out, being a parent means that eventually you will have to tackle some issues that may make you uncomfortable and squeamish. I'm already dreading the day when Rollie, calmly observing me change or bathe Elsa, will ask why she doesn't have a penis. And I get a rash just thinking about when I'll have to explain the facts of life, or answer such questions as, *Did you drink in high school? Did you fool around with guys? What's a Glory Hole?*

Right now I'm grappling with how to explain death. I hadn't really planned out how I was going to have this discussion with Rollie. It just sort of came up and punched me in the face when our fish died.

I didn't think Rollie would notice, but the day after I flushed Mr. Shark down the toilet and thus into the big fishbowl in the sky, Rollie paused in front of our tank.

After studying it for a few seconds, he asked, "Where'd the shark go?"

I froze. Do I tell him the truth, that Mr. Shark was likely attacked by our bully of an Orange Molly, picked at and prodded until he turned pale and I found him floating vertically among the water plants, his dorsal fin shredded like coleslaw? Or do I wimp out and come up with some sugar-coated, cotton-candy spun tale about him swimming away to be with his friends in a beautiful blue lake, his life now full of rainbows and sunshine?

"Uh, he's probably hiding," I said. Like a giant, lying wus.

Rollie stood on his tiptoes, his chubby hands pressed against the glass as he scanned the tank, trying to catch a glimpse of the suddenly timid Bala Shark.

"I can't see him," he said.

"Oh," I said, feeling my scalp prickle as my mind raced. "Well, maybe he's sleeping."

Rollie nodded, accepting this as perfectly reasonable. "Night, night, Shark."

I felt terrible about lying, but really, what could I have said? How do you explain death to a two-year-old? I mean, I've mentioned death in passing plenty of times...in reference to batteries, or worms that have been baked in the sun, curled and black as overdone French fries. But when faced with a question regarding a pet (albeit a lame, neutral pet that Rollie couldn't care less about), I turn into an overprotective, fretful mother hen, paranoid that the mention of death will instantly turn my son into a sobbing mound of jelly.

I realize how stupid it is to harbor such paranoia. Of course he won't have a breakdown as soon as I say the word *Dead*. He might even ask for—and perhaps understand—an explanation. I don't need to include the gory details of the shark's demise. I don't need to say anything like, *The Bala Shark was attacked in his sleep by a bigger, meaner fish, and probably suffered a slow, painful death all alone in the darkest, coldest part of the tank.* Something simple like, *The Bala Shark died and Mommy took him out of the tank, but we can remember him as a nice fish that enjoyed swimming,* would probably be fine.

Another previous uncharted territory we've encountered recently is the barrage of 'why' questions Rollie has begun asking. And because my husband is a chemical engineer, decidedly left-brained and incredibly eager to foster any inquisitiveness our children display, he tries to field every nuance of the why questions Rollie can dish out. I heard him attempt to keep up with the stream of 'whys' the other night, bless his heart:

Rollie: Why did the garbage man come, Dadda?

Jeff: Because today's garbage day.

Rollie: But why did he take our garbage?

Jeff: Because if he didn't, our garbage would keep piling up until it filled up our house.

Rollie: But *why* did he take it?

Jeff: Because it's his job, honey.

Rollie: But why did he take it *away*?

Jeff (*with a slight tone of annoyance creeping into his voice*): Because we left our garbage at the end of the driveway for him.

Rollie: Why did we leave our garbage for him?

Jeff: Rollie, I just told you…if we didn't let him take our garbage, it would pile up and fill up our garage and we wouldn't be able to pull our cars out and go anywhere, and pretty soon our whole house would be filled with garbage, and we'd have flies in our house, and we wouldn't be able to walk around or play with toys or eat dinner or do anything fun because we'd be wading up to our waists in yucky, stinky garbage.

Rollie: ...But why would our garbage pile up and fill our garage?

Jeff (*now sounding really annoyed and definitely not as eager to explain every why question our son can think of*): If we didn't take it to the end of the driveway for the garbage man, we would run out of places to put it.

Rollie: Why would we run out of places to put it?

Jeff (*heaving a giant sigh*): We just would, Rollie. Now let's play baseball.

And with that, my son's line of questioning was redirected into my husband pitching underhand to him for half an hour. Time well spent to avoid having to come up with answers that will satisfy a two-year-old's half-curiosity, half-desire-to-hear-his-own-voice.

I would have handled this conversation differently:

Rollie: Why did the garbage man come?

Me: Because I said so.

Chapter 22
In Summary...

So I'm assuming here that since you've gotten this far in the book, you must have found a few somewhat relatable instances within its pages, something that made you keep reading. I mean, you're a mom...it's not like you have gobs and gobs of time to just pick up a book whenever you please. I am truly honored that you've made time between fulfilling every possible need for at least one child (or two, or so help you God, five) to actually focus your attention to this book.

Maybe you realized that you have a little White Trash residing inside of you, dormant until you popped out a kid or two, and now you, too, have found yourself wandering the automotive section with your shoeless children. Or perhaps you have often wished you had The Switch, and now you can finally crow to your husband that you aren't the only woman out there who would rather pass out on her own side of the bed instead of engaging in anything even resembling sex. Or maybe you've said *Because I said so* to your child waaaay more often than you thought you should, and were starting to feel a little guilty that you weren't offering up a more elaborate explanation to a kid who wanted to know why he couldn't watch *Diego* for the fifth episode in a row.

What I really set out to accomplish is this: To make sure no mother out there feels alone. That no mother ever feels like she's the only one who doesn't whip up a nutritious, four-food-group-representative meal for her picky-as-hell toddler. Or that she's the only one who would rather peruse Craig's list for a pair of barstools than clean the guest bathroom. Or that no other mom has ever lost her cool, yanked her child's arm, burst into tears when her child peed on the floor, or fantasized about pulling a Thelma and Louise after listening to her children have a screaming contest on the car ride home from Target.

There is one final piece of advice I can give you before sending you back into the wild:

Don't Forget To Laugh.

Truly, of all the advice, warnings, adages and cautionary tales I've gleaned over the past few years, Don't Forget To Laugh is the single most valuable lesson I have ever, *ever* learned. Don't forget to look for the sick hilarity in rearing children. Don't forget to find humor in every power-struggle, temper tantrum, public display of defiance, bodily function mishap and unadulterated meltdown. And don't forget about the Big Picture. Sometimes it will require you to take a few deep breaths, or perhaps drink some beer or wine or devour something totally bad for you and therefore completely delicious. Sometimes you will simply have to find your happy place and hang out there for a little while, ignoring your whining, destructive child, the smells of fresh poop overpowering your Fresh Linen scented candle, the messy house, the unmade dinner, the unwashed (and horny) laundry. Don't worry. It'll all be there when you decide to return from your mental getaway.

And when you *do* return, just take it all in and smile. Chances are, you will get a big, chocolate-smeared, snotty-faced smile right back.

Extra Laughs From Online

The following excerpts were taken from my blog, also entitled *Motherhood Is Easy*. And if any of you have ever felt like you were *this* close to beating your children with the nearest object, even if it ended up being a tube of toothpaste, I highly recommend starting a blog instead. It gives you a sense of removal from the chaos, and a little perspective, and if you hang onto it, you'll have something to show your kids when they're older, in case they don't believe you when you tell them what monsters they used to be.

Enjoy!

Size Matters

So the other day I'm giving Elsa a bath while my husband Jeff is about to take a shower with Rollie. I hear them in the water closet, where Jeff is coaxing Rollie into using the potty before getting into the shower. Jeff cheers, indicating that Rollie's finally peeing, and I hear Rollie say, "Dadda, you have a *big* penis."

"Thank you," Jeff replies. An automatic response, I'm sure. What guy wouldn't want to hear someone telling him he's got a big wang? Even if it is coming from his own two-year-old son.

Then Rollie says, "My penis is small."

"That's because *you're* small," Jeff assures him. "You have small hands, and small feet, too. Someday it will be big."

"Big like Dadda's."

"Probably."

They emerge from the water closet, Jeff with a big grin on his face, no doubt basking in my son's observation. I just shake my head, grateful that Jeff is the one to field Rollie's first discovery of other people's genitalia.

To be honest, for some reason I feel like a weirdo discussing my son's penis with him. Why is that? I'm a grown woman, for crying out loud. It's not like I haven't seen a penis before. I've gotten to know one in particular fairly well. We're on a first name basis, we've had some good times. We send each other Christmas cards.

The thing is, I feel like an impostor when my son asks me about that specific region of his body. I feel like I'm a salesman explaining a product and its function when I've never owned one, used one or even seen one before. I guess it's because I don't have one myself. All my knowledge is second-hand, so

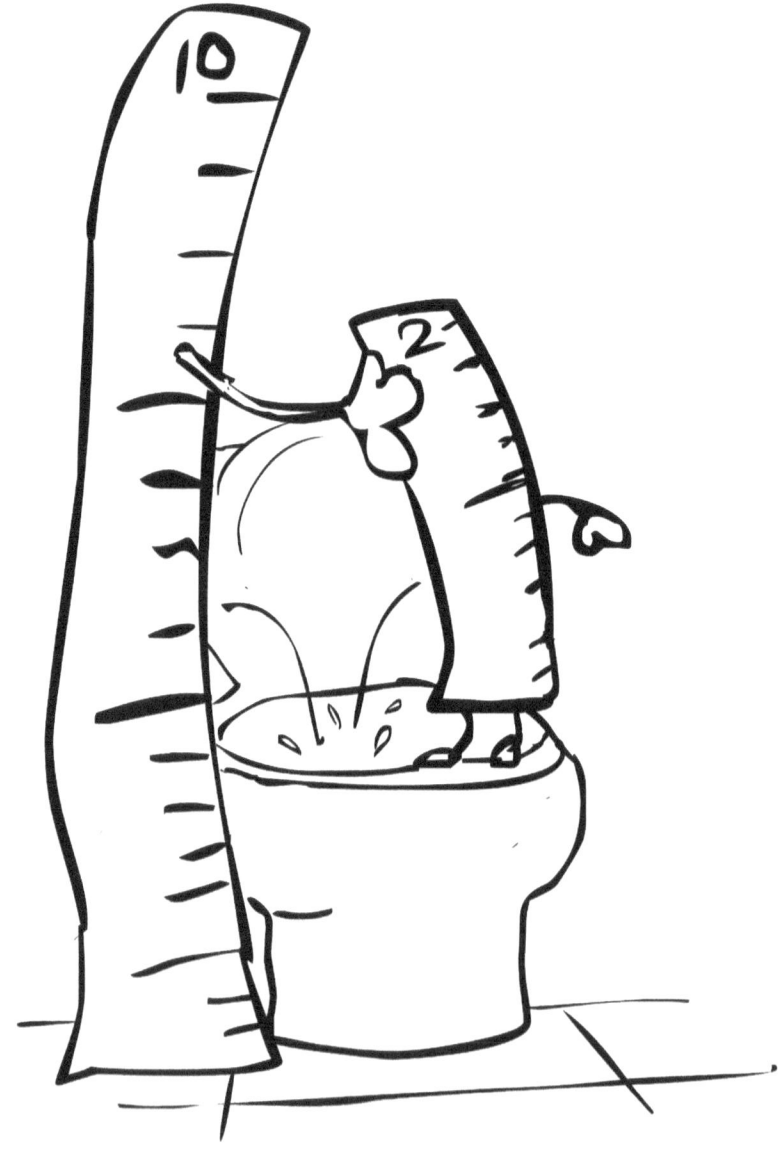

to speak.

Which is ridiculous, really. I *do* know how it works, what it's for, its likes and dislikes....Am I dreading the day when my son stops asking questions about it? When he's got everything figured out just fine, thank you, and I'll be left wondering what exactly he's using it for?

That's when I have to stop myself and realize that he's just two. There'll be plenty of time for all kinds of discussions that will be embarrassing for both of us. For now I'll just sit back and try not to laugh when my son notices that his father has a big penis. Soon the day will come when Elsa tells me I have big boobs. And all I'll be able to do is beam and say, "Thank you!"

Mother By Numbers

Time Rollie woke up yesterday morning: 5:23

Number of blueberries I put on his breakfast plate: 18

Number of blueberries he actually ate: 3

Number of his blueberries I ate: 15

Number of balls I pitched to him during *The Today Show*: 21

Number of times I told him to get off of Elsa or he'll squish her: 12

Number of times I asked him if he had to use the potty: 10

Number of times I asked him if he was *sure* he didn't have to use the potty: 10

Number of times he actually *sat* on the potty: 3

Number of time he actually went *in* the potty: 0

Number of times he peed directly onto the *floor*: 1

Number of towels I used to clean up the mess: 2

Number of pacifiers scattered around the house for Baby Elsa: 4

Number of pacifiers I was able to locate: 0

Number of minutes Elsa spent half-heartedly crying because I couldn't find her pacifier: 7

Number of times I contemplated getting my tubes tied: 6

Number of episodes of *Ni-Hao Kai-Lan* Rollie watched: 2

Number of times Rollie climbed in Elsa's crib: 3

Number of time Rollie climbed into Elsa's crib with Elsa in it: 2

Number of times I threatened to spank Rollie's bottom: 16

Number of times I actually spanked Rollie's bottom: 2

Number of times I *should* have spanked Rollie's bottom: at least 20

Number of times I thought to myself, "Calgon, take me away!": 9

Number of years since I've actually seen that commercial: like, 18, and I finally get it.

Number of minutes my husband was late coming home from work: 90

Number of seconds he was in the door before I threw the kids at him and hid: 2

Number of times Rollie got out of bed after being tucked in: 4

Number of times I sang *Little Rollie* to him: 3

Number of *Family Guy* episodes Jeff and I watched after the kids were finally sleeping: 2

Number of beers I drank while watching *Family Guy*: 1.5

Number of M&M's I ate while drinking beer and watching *Family Guy*: approximately 47

Time I went to bed: 9:43

Number of times I got out of bed to settle down Elsa: 4

Number of times I got out of bed to stop the dog from snoring: 1

Number of times I elbowed Jeff to stop *him* from snoring: 2

Time Rollie woke up today: 5:20

Public Displays Of Correction

Here's one for you.

My entourage and I are at the mall the other day, and I stop at the restroom in one of the department stores (the ones in the foodcourt skeeve me out....I guess because they smell like burgers and the floor is always wet and dotted with sopping globs of TP).

Anyway, I'm sitting on the porcelain throne, doing my thing, and Rollie decides to get down from the sit-and-stand and wander around the handicapped stall (I feel bad taking the big stall, but a.) how often do I really see a wheelchair-bound person in the restroom anyway? and b.) I feel like I'm handicapped in a sense, because I usually only have one arm free and usable...sort of like an amputee but without the phantom-limb syndrome.).

Rollie peeks in the garbage bin, runs his hands along the stall wall, kicks at the door, all the stuff that boys his age do when they're bored and trapped inside a public restroom with their mothers. And I'm doing a sort of running commentary the entire time:

Rollie, don't touch that please, it's dirty. Rollie, no kicking, okay? Rollie, let's leave that alone please. Rollie, Hon, come over here please. Rollie, those are toilet seat covers, we don't need any more right now. Rollie, don't touch the latch, okay? I don't want the door to open yet. Rollie don't look under there—that's rude.

Remember, I'm slightly incapacitated at the time of these instructions—sitting on the toilet with my pants down. I have to be as polite as possible with these orders...God forbid he decide to go right on peering beneath the wall and into the adjoining stall. The poor lady with the crooked toes and orthopedic sandals would not find my child nearly as adorable as I do.

He's doing a good job of listening to my borderline-pleas to obey. That is until he discovers the toilet paper:

Rollie, put that down, please. Rollie, you don't need any toilet paper. Rollie, please stop unrolling that. Rollie, listen to me. Stop. That. Rollie.

Meanwhile, Rollie has grasped the end of the roll and proceeded to spin slowly around and around, a long sheet of toilet paper wrapping itself around his middle like a python squeezing a giant, disobedient rat. And all I can do is watch. I'm still sitting, now unable to grab the toilet paper my son is unraveling. He's out of my reach, and I don't want to sit there and yell at him. It's so damn echo-y in this bathroom, which is tucked away in a quiet, sleepy corner of a department store, the door propped open so anyone trying to shop for over-priced, 500-thread count sheets will hear me screaming at my kid to stop unrolling the freaking toilet paper and get over here Right Now.

So what do I do? I take a picture of him with my cell phone. So I can remember this moment and make sure I strap Rollie in his seat before I assume such a vulnerable position next time.

Moms' Motivational Posters

Ever see those Motivational Posters that seem to be part of every generic office-job's decor (along with artificial ficus trees and putty-colored cubical desks)? You know, they have pictures of snow-capped mountains or hot-air balloons with captions like 'Endurance' and 'Inspiration' with corny definitions? Well, I've come up with a few of my own, specially designed for the mothers of small children....

Baby Gap: Because My Infant Daughter Needs A Thirty-Dollar Pair Of Low-Rise, Boot-Cut Jeans.

Potty Training: The Reason Tile Floors Were Invented.

Dog Food: Sometimes It's Better Than What Mommy Put On Your Plate.

Ni-Hao Kai-Lan: Five Episodes In A Row Is Never Enough.

Boogers: Hey, At Least They're Eating *Something!*

Baby Sisters: Nature's Speed-Bumps.

Matchbox Cars: The Eleventh Plague.

Goldfish Crackers: Still Good After 8 Months Between Two Couch Cushions.

Pacifiers: A Silicon Plug In The Dam Of Mommy's Sanity.

Teething: Finally, Nursing Is Exciting!

Toenail Polish: Someday It Will Look Nice. But Not Today. Or Tomorrow.

Carpeting: Your Child's Wall-To-Wall Napkin.

Wading Pools: The Greatest Invention Of All Time.

Backwash: Even If It *Is* Your Own Son, It's Still Gross.

Grapes: So They *Do* Turn Into Raisins After Baking For Two Weeks Wedged Inside A Carseat Crevice!

Bubblegum: Eventually It Comes Out The Other End.

I'll Never Leave Your Pizza Burnin'

All I wanted today was some leftover pizza.

Was that too much to ask? A nice, lukewarm, slightly soggy slice of pizza and a somewhat cold can of Diet Coke. And some time in front of the computer.

Things were on their way to working out nicely. All I had to do was get the kids to take naps—something I was certain would happen based on their eye-rubbing, bi-polar demeanors, and the fact that they'd both been up since 5:45. So certain was I that they were minutes away from crashing that I even optimistically pulled my pizza from the fridge, placed it on some foil and stuck it in the toaster oven. I would soon be dining and writing in peace and quiet.

Except that Elsa was having a total freak-out in her crib after I put her down. I think she banged her face on the railing, but I can't be sure. Lately, whenever I put her in the crib when she doesn't want to be there (like, all the time), she kneels in front of the bars, grabs onto them like a wrongfully imprisoned captive, and wails. Only I think she may have gotten too big for her britches and actually tried to pull up, thus hitting her chubby, tear-streaked face on the wooden bars.

This happened while I was trying to get Rollie some lunch. I've been employing this new discipline technique with Rollie (which I'm sure you'll be hearing about soon), and part of the idea is to give him choices throughout the day so he feels like he's got some sort of control over his life (unlike Mommy, who feels like she has absolutely no control over anything whatsoever, except for possibly her bladder). So the choice he was grappling with at the moment was if he wanted to take a nap now, or eat his lunch first and then take a nap. He chose to eat first. But that was part of the deal. To actually EAT.

Apparently he didn't get that part. Because as I returned from settling

Elsa back down (ie, loosening her Kung Fu grip on her crib bars, popping her pacifier back into her mouth, replacing her horizontally in her crib and rubbing her back until she stopped hyperventilating and passed out), Rollie wasn't upholding his end of the deal. Oh no. I entered the kitchen just in time to see his peanut butter and jelly sandwich sail through the air and land at our dog's feet. And before I could snatch it up and cram the sandwich into his sweet little mouth (thus abiding by the Five-Second Rule), our dog gobbled it up.

Without a word, I snapped Rollie from his booster chair and hauled him into his room for some Time Out (also abiding by the new discipline technique—calmly placing the offender in Time Out until he's ready to behave like a human being—meaning that Rollie will be in Time Out until he's twenty-five).

Unfortunately, this new technique does not coincide well with Potty Training.

I realized my mistake as soon as I closed his door. I barged back into Rollie's room to see him lying on his tummy, a dark spot spreading across the carpet beneath him.

He looked up, eyes wide, and said, "I went pee-pee, Mommy."

I closed my eyes, breathed in deeply, began counting to ten...and smelled burning pizza. Sigh.

Eventually they both took naps. And I had a bowl of cereal for lunch. But at least I got in some peace and quiet time. Somehow, that always eclipses everything, doesn't it?

Putting The Pee In Developmental Milestones

So my kids have made it past two major developmental milestones: Rollie is peeing standing up, and Elsa is crawling.

Now, taken separately, these two things are celebratory. Finally, I don't have to hear Elsa scream in frustration, trapped in her figure-four leg-lock, unable to travel the thirty inches to reach the toy she desperately wants. She can just get up on her hands and knees and go. And Rollie, my darling son, has discovered the unadulterated joy of aiming his stream of pee to obliterate a square of TP in the toilet. The next step is actually letting me know he has to go without me asking every five seconds. Oh, happy day that will be.

But when these two accomplishments are melded together, it spells complete and utter disaster.

The scenario this morning: Rollie tearing through the house, hollering that he wants a diaper—my cue to usher him into the bathroom.

Me: Come on, Rollie, let's go pee-pee.

Rollie: No, I want a Diaper!

Me: You just need to use the potty.

Rollie: No.

Me (*employing the brilliant method of offering up two choices to trick a kid into thinking he gets any kind of say in his life...usually works well except that oftentimes Rollie will still opt for Door Number Three: His Way*): Do you want to sit or stand to go pee-pee?

Rollie (*who thankfully realizes this is not a drill*): I want to stand.

Yay. He's not going to pee on the floor *this* round. I strategically position his plastic potty chair in front of the toilet so he can stand on it, help

him with his shorts and Thomas undies, toss a crumpled tissue into the bowl, and hold him in place, his belly protruding forward so that he himself cannot see his wiener, only the stream of pee emitting from it and splashing below.

(Side note: Yes, I realize that I still sometimes call a Penis a Wiener. I don't know when I will finally behave like the 31-year-old woman I actually am and start using the anatomically correct terminology. I think I will also have a problem saying Vulva, but I'll worry about that later. Much, much later.)

So just as I'm feeling all smug and triumphant, like maybe, just *maybe*, I've bought Rollie his last box of size 6 diapers, I hear the little *smack smack smacking* of baby hands on ceramic tile.

I turn and see Elsa, chubby-faced and smiling, making a bee-line for us.

"No, no, Elsa," I say. Because I already know where she's headed.

She pauses only long enough to smile even wider before continuing onward.

"Don't come over here, Elsa," I say.

Smack smack smack.

"Elsa. Stop, Honey."

Smack smack smack. Man, she's quick.

"What's Baby Elsa doing?" Rollie asks, though he's still engrossed with peeing on the tissue.

"She's not listening to Mommy," I say. "Elsa, no, no."

By now Elsa has crawled behind me and is now on her hands and knees, looking up at the toilet looming above her. She contemplates it for a moment, then lifts one doughy hand up and grasps the rim.

Keep in mind that I'm still holding onto Rollie, who for some reason doesn't stand under his own power when he pees. It's like helping someone who's heavily intoxicated. If I let him go, he'll pee all over the place.

Elsa seems to know my dilemma, because she now reaches up with her other hand and pulls herself onto her knees, watching with great interest as Rollie continues to go. The pee stream is inches away from her curious little face. One move on his part and she'll get a golden shower. Maybe that'll teach her.

"*Elsaaaaa*," I lower my voice to mimic Jeff's—one discouraging word from him and Elsa is usually reduced to a quivering pile of baby-fat.

But instead of bursting into tears, Elsa leans forward and sticks her hand right into the toilet.

"Aaah!" I shriek, releasing Rollie and diving for Elsa.

"Momma!" Rollie teeters on the potty seat for a second before standing up straight, pee running down his leg and onto the potty seat.

I lug a squirming Elsa to the sink. At least I'm able to wash her hands before she decides to put them in her mouth. Sometimes you've gotta rejoice in the little victories.

WhyAskWhyAskWhyAskWhy

It's finally begun.

We've officially entered the 'Why' stage.

I guess we've been in it for a week or two...maybe longer...who knows really—all my days are blurring together in one thick, fuzzy fog of answering Rollie's questions every five freaking seconds.

I must say, being asked 'why' about absolutely everything is kind of eye-opening. I mean, Rollie is asking some pretty heavy questions, the kind of questions you would expect to ponder if you'd been taking some serious psychotropic substances and were sprawled on someone's front lawn, gazing up at the stars and just letting your mind *go*, man.

We were all walking the dog the other evening, and it started to rain. Jeff pulled the canopy over Rollie's seat in the stroller, and Rollie, who had been zoning in the front seat, almost asleep, suddenly perked up.

Rollie: Why are you doing that, Dadda?

Jeff: Because it's starting to rain.

Rollie: Why is it starting to rain, Dadda?

Jeff: Because the clouds are full of water and it's too heavy to hold any more.

Rollie: Why is the water too heavy?

Jeff: Because water molecules are starting to coalesce and condense into liquid—this makes them more dense than the air, and then the liquid water drops to the ground as rain. (*I know...kind of an esoteric answer for a two-year-old to wrap his little head around, but I suppose it's better than just saying, be quiet and go to sleep,*

Discovery of the Atom

which is how I felt like answering.)

I'm pretty sure this is how the atom was discovered. Newton was hanging out with his two-year-old son, and the son kept asking why, breaking down every answer into a smaller question, until eventually Newton looked at his son and said, *There are no more answers. We have finally arrived at the last possibly way to break down this subject into its tiniest part.* Hence, the atom! (Oh wait...Jeff just told me that the components that make up the atom are smaller than the atom itself. Quarks...Electrons...all that stuff that I've completely blocked out since eleventh grade Chemistry class...which would probably explain the disparity between Jeff's responses and mine to Rollie's aforementioned rain question....)

I'm having a different experience with the 'why's' Rollie is sending my way.

I was ushering him into the bathroom to go pee, bribing him with the promise that I had to go as well, since for some reason the prospect of peeing as a family entices him to use the toilet. Like a little duckling, he followed me into the bathroom and pulled out his plastic potty, then asked if we could cross the streams, since that is how he pees with Jeff (my apologies if this is entirely too much information....).

Me: Oh, I can't cross streams, Honey. Only Dadda can cross streams with you.

Rollie: Why can't you cross streams, Momma?

Me: Well, because that's not the way Mommy goes pee-pee.

Rollie: Why is that not the way you go pee-pee, Momma?

Me (*thinking, oh boy...here we go*): Because Mommy doesn't have a penis.

Rollie: Why doesn't you have a penis, Momma?

Me: Because I'm a girl.

Rollie (*eyeing me somewhat suspiciously*): Can I see your Not Penis, Momma?

Me: Well, there's really nothing to see, Baby.

Rollie: But why can't you cross streams, Momma?

Me: I think I just told you.

Rollie: But *why*?

Me: Well...girls go pee-pee differently from boys. It's just how we're made.

And before he could ask one more why question, forcing me to delve into the anatomically correct terminology for our corresponding parts, I swiftly changed the subject to his new Thomas the Train underwear.

But his curiosity in my Not Penis was only temporarily squelched. As I escorted him into Starbucks the other day to use the restroom, he asked me out of the blue: "Do you not have a penis, Momma?"

Me: That's right, I don't.

Rollie: And you can't cross the streams?

Me: Nope.

Rollie: But you can still go pee-pee?

Me: Sure can.

Rollie: Why can you still go pee-pee Momma?

Me: Because I had a lot to drink today.

Rollie: Why did you have a lot to drink today?

Me: Because I'm extra thirsty from answering all your questions.

Rollie: Why are you extra thirsty?

Me: I just told you, Love.

Rollie: Why did you just told me?

Me: ...I don't know.

I understand that he doesn't in fact *want* to know why to every single question; he's pretty fascinated that he can dictate the course of an entire conversation, get some attention *and* hear his own voice all at the same time. So I guess I'll have to keep supplying him with answers, feeding his burgeoning and insatiable curiosity, until I either get such cotton-mouth I can no longer move my lips, or we discover a new subatomic particle and make millions of dollars....

Let There Be Lightning McQueen

I hate to say it, but I've been feeling a little inferior lately. To my husband, I mean. He's just a lot better than I am at answering Rollie's questions. I guess his Chemical Engineering degree is finally paying off.

But instead of wallowing in a pool of English degree self-pity, I'm trying to embrace Rollie's latest phase. I'm trying to field the bombardment of 'why's' with enthusiasm and understanding. I'm trying my best to answer his questions correctly, using words and phrases he should understand, and incorporating visual aides and demonstrations when possible. And it's not going so well.

This morning I called him to the back door so he could see the sunrise. The clouds were like county-fair cotton candy, steam rose from the lake where wading birds stood silent and still. Everything was wet with dew. Even our moldy porch furniture was beautiful in the muted morning light.

He stopped harassing Elsa long enough to trot over to me and gaze out the back door at the splendorous dawn.

Me: See how pretty the clouds look, Rol?

Rollie: Where's the sun, Momma?

Me: The sun's still sleeping.

Rollie: Why is the sun sleeping?

Me: Well, he's not really *sleeping*. He's just sort of...hiding.

Rollie: Why is he hiding?

Me: It's just not time for him to be up yet.

Rollie: Where is he, Momma?

The Science of Motherhood

Me: Behind those trees.

Rollie: Why is he behind those trees?

Me (*studying the tree line and realizing the sun is still well below the horizon*): Well, he's not actually *behind* the trees. He's kind of...below them.

Rollie: Why is he kind of below them?

Me: Well, because the earth is round and spinning, and it hasn't really turned enough for us to face the sun yet. (*Nice answer, Copernicus.*)

Rollie: Why?

And then I had a bolt of inspiration. My mind flashed to my brief stint as a tutor, and the phrase *Teachable Moment* illuminated in my brain in big, neon letters.

Me: Come on, Rollie. I want to show you something.

I brought him into his bedroom and selected a soccer ball from his overflowing basket of balls of every size, shape and sport.

Me (*holding the ball up for him to see*): Now, let's pretend that this is Earth. Earth is where we live. See how it's round?

Rollie: Why is it round?

Me: We'll get to that. Now, (*I grab a Lego chicken from Rollie's play table*) let's pretend this is you. (*I hold the chicken on the ball.*) See? You're standing on Earth.

Rollie (*scratching his head*): Why am I a chicken?

Me: I think you're missing the point, but that's okay.

Rollie: Why am I missing the point?

Me (*determined to soldier on*): Now, let's pretend your Lightning McQueen flashlight is the sun. (*I flip on the switch and aim the beam at the soccer ball.*) See how the light is only on one side the ball? That's like daytime. And see how the chicken isn't in the light? That's because it's nighttime. For the chicken. I mean, for you.

Rollie: Why is it...why is it nighttime for the chicken?

Me: Ah-ha, because the earth hasn't *turned* enough to get the chicken into the light. But watch this. (*I turn the ball so that the chicken is basking in the heat of the Lightning McQueen flashlight.*) Now the chicken is in the sun. See? It's morning! The ball—I mean—*Earth* has turned far enough so that the light is on the chicken. See? Like the sun coming up in the morning. Get it?

Rollie: ....Can we do something else, Momma?

I sat there on the floor with the Lightning McQueen flashlight clutched in one hand, the soccer ball in the other and a Lego chicken between my fingers, and I instantly felt like a mad scientist or a crazy math teacher. What the hell am I doing? Why am I making it so f-ing complicated? Now I get why the phrase, *Because I said so*, is truly the best tool a parent can use. Right up there with coffee.

I think from now on I will stick to my comfort zone of answers:

a.) Ask Dad

b.) Because I said so

c.) Because God made it that way

d.) I don't know

And my new, favorite, what-the-hell-did-our-parents-do-before-the-Internet answer:

e.) Let's look it up on Wikipedia

Is That Hair Gel?

The other day I found Elsa alone in her room playing contentedly with a piece of yarn. I swooped down and kissed her on her fuzzy head... and discovered that her hair was plastered down in front, and stiff as lemon meringue.

"What the..." I examined her hair, but besides the odd texture, nothing else seemed abnormal. She didn't smell like maple syrup or hair spray. I couldn't find any other evidence that would point to her just having landed headfirst into a puddle of slime. Just a streak of stiff, slightly sticky hair.

"What happened to you?" I asked her. To which she replied by looking up at me with those huge blue eyes and wrinkling her nose in a grin.

"Why is your hair all gross?" I asked. She grinned again.

I grabbed a baby wipe from her changing table and tried to remove the mystery substance from her hair, but she squirmed and whined and arched her back, eager to get back to that exciting piece of yarn.

"Hang on a minute," I said, trying to wipe her hair clean. Still she struggled. Why do babies freak out when you're trying to clean them? Good grief, you'd think I was trying to pull off her nose with a pair of pliers.

I gave up and tossed the wipe, then started picking up some of her toys. And then I heard Rollie in his room. Playing. And singing. And then... sneezing.

"Bless you!" I yelled.

He didn't reply, but a few seconds later he ran into Elsa's room, where Elsa had abandoned her yarn and was now chewing on a sock. Before I could say or do anything, Rollie leaned down and gently rubbed his nose on Elsa's head. Then he sprinted from the room.

Well, that explains the mystery goo.

"Rollie!" I followed him into his room.

"Yes, Momma?" he asked. He was lying on his stomach, carefully assembling a Noah's Ark puzzle. (Any time you walk in on your child doing something with a Biblical Theme—a Tower of Babel coloring book, a Red Sea-scape, a mosaic of The Last Supper, a Nativity diarama—you can safely assume you've got yourself a hidden crime scene somewhere else in the house. Go check your fish tank or your toilets...it's likely that something incongruous is floating around in there.)

"Rollie...you don't use Baby Elsa's head as a tissue." *That's a new one.*

"Okay."

"If you need to wipe your nose, use a tissue from the bathroom."

"But they're all gone."

Of course! That is the only possible explanation for why you'd be wiping your snot on your sister!

"Okay, well, we'll get you some more at the store. You can use toilet paper until we go to Publix."

"Toilet paper goes in the potty," he said.

"I know, but today you need to use it on your nose, too."

"Why?"

"Because we're out of tissues."

"Why?"

"Because I forgot to buy them last time."

"Why did you forget to buy them last time?"

"Probably because you were distracting me with your grocery store antics. Now stop blowing your nose on Baby Elsa."

Finally he seemed satisfied with my answers and focused his attention back to his puzzle. But I was left wondering how many really disgusting things he does when I'm not looking...how many stains and marks and sticky spots on the floor are his doing? Here I've been blaming the dog for sneezing on the wall or leaving dog biscuit crumbs on the carpet, when all along my own son was the likely culprit. I've caught him wiping his mouth on the couch, his hands on the bathmat...I've seen him throw chewing gum on the ground and shove raisins into the little hole beneath his carseat buckle. Where he picks up these habits I'll never know. I'm not the model of anal fastidiousness by any means, but I use a tissue when I need one, and I usually throw garbage where it belongs (exception—my purse has served as a trash can on numerous occasions).

But lesson learned. From now on I'll be sure to have a supply of Kleenex for my son. Otherwise things could get messy. Especially once Elsa's hair gets longer.

Magic Mom

My son must think I'm magical.

It's really the only explanation for my clairvoyance, my super-human strength, my omnipotence, and the pair of eyes residing on the back of my head.

I utter something like, "I should probably put the vacuum cleaner away or you'll start climbing on it," and he'll stare at me as if to say, *How did you know that's exactly what I intended to do the second you left the room?* Or we'll be in the car, I'll look in my rearview mirror and see him about to stick his foot in his baby sister's face and I'll bark, "Rollie, put your foot down." He looks up, startled and bewildered, thinking, *How the hell did she know that? She didn't even turn around!*

I announce that he's tired and he shakes his head, even though he's rubbing his eyes and staggering like a battered boxer, and deep down he's telling himself that he's exhausted but must not under any circumstances let me know I'm right. He runs into his room and shuts the door and I knock, telling him to sit on the potty. He's a deer in headlights, always flabbergasted that I am more in tune with his excretory system than he is. Yes, my son can't even think about taking a crap without me right there with him, telling him he'd better use the bathroom so I don't have to change yet another diaper.

I can find any toy, open any door, reach things and cook things and read anything I see. I am faster, bigger and stronger that he is, and I know the answer to almost everything. It's no wonder he seeks me out when he's hurt, or frightened, or just needs a hug. And also no wonder he hides from me when he's done something wrong—I must already know the crime and am busy preparing a punishment.

I wish I were indeed magical, that I could clean up his booster seat

with a wriggle of my nose instead of fifty scrubs with a damp paper towel. Or I could keep him in his bed with a simple spell instead of two night lights, a white noise machine and a baby gate. I wish I could protect him with pixie dust, I wish I could keep him innocent and healthy and happy with enchantment charms and magic wands and special potions. But mostly I wish I could keep up the appearance that I am indeed magic. I wish he would always see me as all-powerful, all-seeing, all-knowing. I wish he would always see me through the eyes of a wondering child and not the eyes of a jaded adult.

I wish.

Author photos by Natalie Law

About the Author

Originally from New Jersey, Rebekah Hunter Scott attended Florida State University, where she got both her B.A. in creative writing and her husband. After several years of corporate day-jobs and moonlighting as a writer, she now spends her days with her two children and writes when they're napping.

Rebekah is a member of the Florida Writers Association, has been published in *The Flagler Review,* and won first place for short fiction in *The Storyteller's* People's Choice Awards, Spring 2008. Her fiction is also featured in the anthology *From Our Family To Yours* (Peppertree Press), and *Writing Is Easy* (ClearView Press, Inc., Spring 2010). She is also a contributing writer to *The Creekline* newspaper. She lives in St. Augustine with her family.

www.motherhoodiseasy.com

www.motherhoodiseasy.blogspot.com

www.rebekahhunterscott.com

www.ingramcontent.com/pod-product-compliance
Lightning Source LLC
Chambersburg PA
CBHW031248290426
44109CB00012B/479